ABOUT BRITAIN NO. 2

WESSEX

WITH A PORTRAIT BY

GEOFFREY GRIGSON

PUBLISHED FOR THE
FESTIVAL OF BRITAIN OFFICE
COLLINS
14 ST JAMES'S PLACE
LONDON

THE ABOUT BRITAIN GUIDES

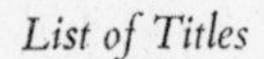

List of Titles

1. WEST COUNTRY. *Portrait by* Geoffrey Grigson.
Cornwall: Devonshire: Somerset: Gloucestershire: N.W. Wiltshire.

2. WESSEX. *Portrait by* Geoffrey Grigson.
S.E. Wiltshire: Dorset: Hampshire: Isle of Wight.

3. HOME COUNTIES. *Portrait by* R. S. R. Fitter.
Sussex: Surrey: Kent: London: Middlesex: East Berkshire: S.E. Buckinghamshire: Hertfordshire: S.W. Essex.

4. EAST ANGLIA. *Portrait by* R. H. Mottram.
N.E. Essex: Suffolk: Norfolk: Cambridgeshire: Huntingdonshire: Soke of Peterborough: Holland (Lincs.)

5. CHILTERNS TO BLACK COUNTRY. *Portrait by* W. G. Hoskins.
West Berkshire: Oxfordshire: North Buckinghamshire: Bedfordshire: Northamptonshire (excluding Corby area): Warwickshire: Worcestershire: Staffordshire.

6. SOUTH WALES AND THE MARCHES. *Portrait by* W. J. Gruffydd.
Pembrokeshire: Caermarthenshire: Glamorgan: Monmouthshire: Brecknockshire: Cardiganshire: Radnorshire: Herefordshire.

7. NORTH WALES AND THE MARCHES. *Portrait by* W. J. Gruffydd.
Montgomeryshire: Merionethshire: Caernarvonshire: Anglesey: Denbighshire: Flintshire: Shropshire: Cheshire.

8. EAST MIDLANDS AND THE PEAK. *Portrait by* W. G. Hoskins.
Leicestershire: Lincolnshire (except Holland): Rutland: Corby area of Northamptonshire: Nottinghamshire: Derbyshire.

9. LANCASHIRE AND YORKSHIRE. *Portrait by* Leo Walmsley.
Most of Yorkshire: Lancashire except Lake District.

10. LAKES TO TYNESIDE. *Portrait by* Sid Chaplin.
Cumberland: Westmorland: Lake District (Lancashire): Part of North Riding (Yorkshire): Durham: Northumberland: Isle of Man.

11. LOWLANDS OF SCOTLAND. *Portrait by* John R. Allan.

12. HIGHLANDS AND ISLANDS OF SCOTLAND. *Portrait by* Alastair M. Dunnett.

13. NORTHERN IRELAND. *Portrait by* E. Estyn Evans.

The Relief Maps used for the covers and jackets of these books were designed and produced by Geographical Projects Ltd.

Produced by A. N. Holden & Co. Ltd., London, and printed in England by Sun Printers Ltd., London and Watford. Published by Wm. Collins Sons & Co., Ltd., in 1951.

Avebury, Wiltshire: blocks of sarsen in the great ritual circle, built about 1800 B.C. (see page 10).

CONTENTS

Page 7 PORTRAIT OF WESSEX *by Geoffrey Grigson*

67 THE TOURS

80 GAZETTEER *by Geoffrey Grigson*

LIST OF PHOTOGRAPHERS

3 Avebury: *British Travel Association*
5 Old Sarum: *British Travel Association*
7 Wiltshire Downland: *The Times*
8 Badbury Rings: *Aerofilms*
9 Maiden Castle: *Aerofilms*
11 Harvest on Salisbury Plain: *Picture Post Library*
12 Charmouth: *H. & V. Joel*
13 [COLOUR] West Bay, Dorset: *D. A. Spencer*
15 Lyme Regis: *Architectural Review*
16 Portland quarries: *W. McWilliam*
17 Making fishing-line, Bridport: *Crown Copyright*
18 Chesil Bank: *The Times*
19 The figure of George III, Weymouth: *Aerofilms*
21 [COLOUR] Abbotsbury Swannery: *Keystone*

LIST OF PHOTOGRAPHERS (*concluded*)

22 Swanage: *Val Doone.* Corfe: *H. & V. Joel.* Shaftesbury: *H. & V. Joel*
24 Corfe Castle: *British Travel Association*
25 Lulworth Cove: *The Times*
27 The Needles: *Aerofilms*
29 [COLOUR] Salisbury Cathedral: *Robert Atkinson* for *New Naturalist*
30 Bloxworth Heath: *The Times*
31 The New Forest: *J. Allan Cash*
33 Fishing on the Test: *The Field*
34 Milking on the Hosier system: *Farmers Weekly*
35 Milk churns: *United Dairies*
36 Portchester: *Aerofilms*
37 Southampton: *Reuter*
38 Bournemouth: *Official Information Bureau, Bournemouth*
39 Yachts at Southsea: *Aerofilms*
40 Navy Day: *The Times*
43 H.M.S. Victory Museum, Portsmouth: *The Times*
45 Purbeck cliff-quarry: *R. E. St Leger-Gordon*
49 Eastbury House: *Country Life*
53 West Dean Church Monument: *F. C. Hedger,*
57 Winchester Cathedral: *British Travel Association*
61 Crichel House: *A. F. Kersting*
65 Stourhead Gardens: *G. Leslie Horn*
67 Salisbury Plain: *H. & V. Joel*
83 Christchurch Priory: *H. & V. Joel*
85 St Mary's Church, E. Lulworth: *A. F. Kersting*
87 Wardour Old Castle: *Country Life*
89 Isle of Wight Steamer: *J. Allan Cash*
90 Lulworth Castle: *H. & V. Joel*

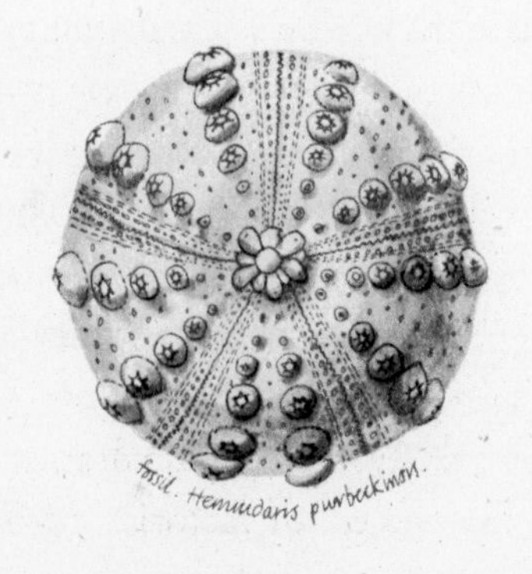

The rampart which surrounds the deserted city of Old Sarum, with the spire of the cathedral of Salisbury or New Sarum beyond.

USING THIS BOOK

THIS GUIDE-BOOK is one of a series 'About Britain,' so we hope, in a new way. Like the others (there are thirteen altogether) it contains many photographs, a map, a gazetteer, and illustrated strip-maps of the most convenient itineraries. And it begins with a portrait of the district—an account of many of the facts about it which are worth knowing and many of the things which are worth seeing.

This does not explain the newness. These guides have been prompted by the Festival of Britain. The Festival shows how the British people, with their energy and natural resources, contribute to civilization. So the guide-books as well celebrate a European country alert, ready for the future, and strengthened by a tradition which you can *see* in its remarkable monuments and products of history and even pre-history. If the country includes Birmingham, Glasgow or Belfast, it includes Stonehenge. If it contains Durham Cathedral, it contains coal mines, iron foundries, and the newest of factories devising all the goods of a developing civilization. If it includes remnants of medieval forest, it includes also the new forests of conifers transforming acres of useless land. It contains art galleries and wild scenery, universities and remote villages, great ports and small fishing harbours, shrines of national sentiment and institutes of scientific research—the past and the present. On the Downs in Wiltshire we can stand on a minute plot of ground on which the Iron Age farmer reaped his corn with a sickle, and watch a few yards away a combine harvester steadily devouring ripe acres of wheat.

What we are as a people, where we have our homes, what we do, what we make—cotton in Lancashire, tin plate in South Wales, cars outside Oxford, mustard or clothes in Norwich, woollens in Bradford —depends all of it upon a thousand national peculiarities, of soil, vegetation, minerals, water, ways of transport, the continuity and the accidents of history.

It is this living country of today which these guide-books emphasize, the place and the people, not only the country of the past or the exquisitely varied landscape of fields and moors and mountains and coast. They are handbooks for the explorer. The aim is to show what Britain is now, in the North, the Midlands and the South, in East Anglia and the West, in Wales, Scotland, Northern Ireland, and to explain something of the why and wherefore. To investigate this Britain the sensible explorer has to take to the roads and the by-roads. This accounts for the itineraries and the strip-maps, which have been devised to guide you, if you need them, as simply, quickly and comprehensively as possible through the districts portrayed by word and illustration in each book.

The Festival of Britain belongs to 1951. But we hope these explorers' handbooks will be useful far beyond the Festival year.

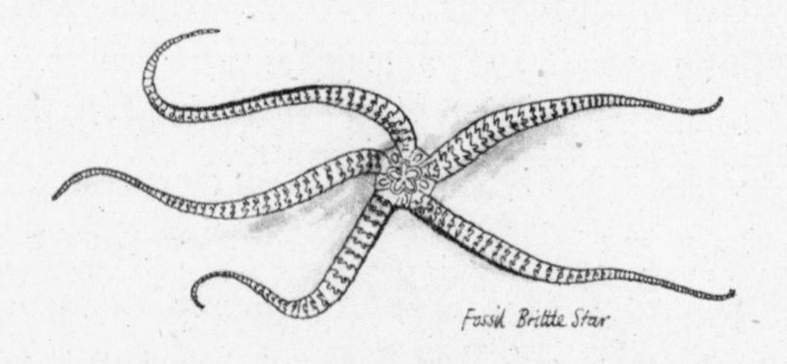

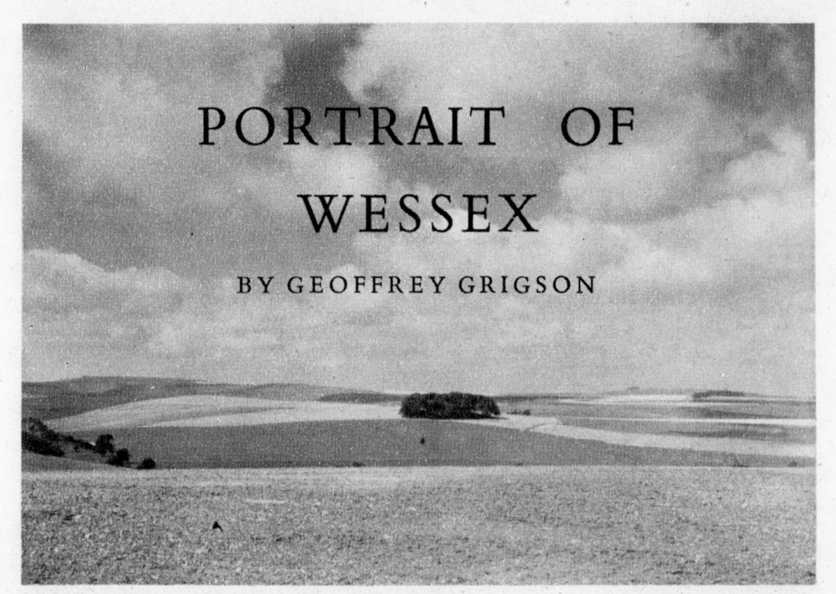

PORTRAIT OF WESSEX

BY GEOFFREY GRIGSON

The downlands of Wiltshire near West Overton.

PERHAPS Wessex[1] suggests place rather than people, a region of country in these days rather than one of people with a common interest or sentiment: Salisbury and the cathedral, Winchester, Dorchester and the scenes of the novels of Thomas Hardy, Cranborne Chase, the New Forest, Salisbury Plain and Stonehenge. The weight of Hardy may have shifted Wessex westward from the plain and from the old capital of the West Saxons at Winchester. But I think we should begin with Stonehenge and the wide plain of subtly linked curves and slopes, of sheep and clouds (though it looks as if the sheep will soon be a memory) associated with valleys of clear streams moving serenely off the chalk. Henry James once went to Stonehenge and felt underneath him 'the pathless vaults beneath the house of history.' History or pre-history (a word unknown to James), the vaults may no longer be so pathless; but it is none the less true to suggest that Wessex is the primal heart of England, if not of Great Britain. The heart is not in the centre of the human body; and the Wessex counties, Hampshire, Wiltshire

1. Wessex for this book comprises Hampshire, Isle of Wight, all of Wiltshire except the north-west fringe by the Cotswolds, a western portion of Berkshire, and all of Dorset. The modern use of Wessex does not correspond to the elastic limits of the ancient kingdom. It will be clear when I am talking of Wessex historically.

Wessex is speckled with prehistoric camps. Badbury Rings in Dorset –

and Dorset, together with the Isle of Wight, broadly face the great thoroughfare of the Channel. They beckon across no great width of sea to France and continental Europe. Hill and valley, light rolling upland and fertile lowland, Wessex has always asked to be invaded and settled from the other side. Whether you are close to Stonehenge, Avebury, Maiden Castle, Wansdyke, the mounds of Old Sarum or far from them, you are never far in Wessex from human history. Man around you has always been up to something. Through several thousand years, in one way and another, he has modified the landscape and made use of the surface. He has scratched the uplands or been a shepherd upon them, his flocks nibbling the landscape clean of scrub; he has ploughed in the valleys, devised harbours along the coast, dug out the stone and clay, and felled the timber.

A geological consideration of Wessex shows, nevertheless, why the heart is no longer the heart. The virtues were not absolute. A thick floor of chalk was laid down below the sea: the chalk curves up from Hampshire through Wiltshire and curves back into Dorset. It forms a round basin, though the rim of the basin is gapped now along the

– and Maiden Castle, near Dorchester, finally stormed by the Romans about A.D. 43.

Channel, the chalk appearing as a ridge in Purbeck and then reappearing in the Isle of Wight. This chalk may determine the greater part of Wessex, the gaps may lead into the gateways of Portsmouth and Southampton Water, and the Isle of Wight may shelter the gateways; but the basin or the tub is filled at the bottom above the chalk with gravel, sand and clay, which lies like a barrier along the coast, producing bog, heath and woodland. Our modern spirit delights in variation of scenery, in alternations of tame and wild, smooth sheepwalk and wilderness; we may think of Wessex first of all in the shape of the Hampshire Downs, Salisbury Plain or the Marlborough Downs or the chalklands of Dorset, but we do not object to the barrenness created by the gravels in the bottom of the tub.

You may remember how Thomas Hardy opens *The Return of the Native* with a sultry account of 'Egdon Heath' – 'a Face upon which Time makes but little impression.' It was 'embrowning' itself moment by moment in a November twilight. Dorset and Hampshire have their share of brown heath to balance the chalk – the heathy country, for instance, east of Dorchester, which Hardy had in mind, and around

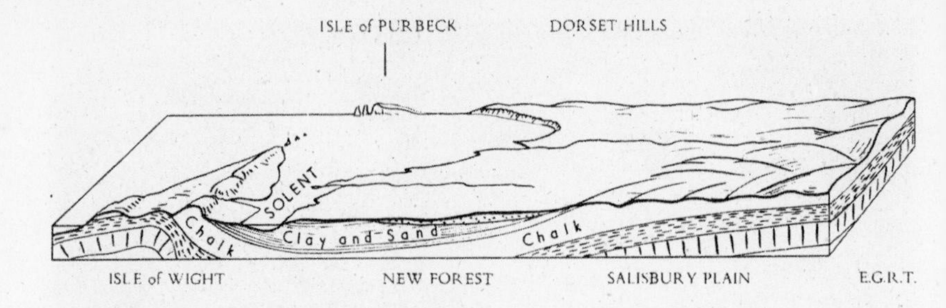

Poole Harbour. If you go by train or by road from Swanage to Wareham and then on to Poole and Bournemouth, you see much heathy, sandy desolation planted with pine or rhododendron. Sands (and clay), too, are the wherefore of the New Forest, tree and pool and bog; and wide patches of bog myrtle which smell resinously and deliciously on a warm spring day as you move east towards the Beaulieu River and Southampton Water. And beyond Southampton Water the New Forest was matched by Bere Forest, round Catherington, most of which has now disappeared. Poverty then at the gate, riches inland and upland, so long as riches came from sheep or farm (though there are sands also in the north of Hampshire which brought the army to Aldershot and – over the Berkshire border – to *Sand*hurst).

Wessex began as the heart, but it lacked the other sources of wealth, coal and iron (iron at least in quantity). The crossing from abroad was longer than the crossing to Kent and into the mouth of the Thames. Only small rivers flowed down from the upland, the Test or the Itchen into Southampton Water, the Avon from Salisbury to Christchurch, and no lengthy navigable Thames was there to give eventual access to a huge area, north, west and south. We have to look at Wessex before these drawbacks began to take charge; for of those early times there is much to examine of the greatest fascination.

AVEBURY AND STONEHENGE

If Wessex was the heart of England, the heart of Wessex must really be centred around Stonehenge and Avebury, the primeval St Paul's and Westminster Abbey of England-before-the-English. Several museums in Wessex reveal much of its earliest story – as at Salisbury, Devizes, Dorchester or the museum at Farnham in Dorset, hidden away in the country just north of the gaunt road from Blandford to Salisbury, which was privately established by General Pitt-Rivers, the pioneer of

Contrasts on Salisbury Plain: the farm borders the aerodrome.

the modern scientific techniques of excavation. But the one I would go to first is none of these: it is the new miniature museum just outside the circle at Avebury. Our knowledge of Avebury and Stonehenge, two of the greatest monuments of antiquity in Europe, may be limited, but religious they certainly were, temples no doubt serving a wide ambit of shepherding and settlement. The museum at Avebury does not only explain, as far as it can be explained, the temple itself: it is also filled with the fruits of excavating a Neolithic 'camp' on the inconspicuous Windmill Hill, just to the west. You cannot get to Windmill Hill by car, but it is worth walking from the Avebury-Swindon road up to the summit – 'a pretty round apex, the turf soft as velvet,' with air 'extremely fragrant,' as William Stukeley described it 200 years ago. It is worth it less for what you can see – a couple of barrows and two or three hundred yards of grassy rampart and the ditches lately excavated – than because you will be standing inside the camp in a site still older than Avebury down below; in fact on one of the earliest farming sites of Great Britain, the first of its kind to be excavated and understood, and one which has given its name to a phase of Neolithic culture. Windmill Hill was used some 4,400 years ago by farmers who crossed over from the chalklands of Northern France. It was not a dwelling-site, but a corral, so it appears, where they rounded up their

Dorset coast: looking towards Golden Cap from the beach at Charmouth.

herds and flocks in the autumn to slaughter the surplus animals. In the museum are the bones of the people themselves, and of the cattle, sheep and pigs they reared, the deer antlers they cultivated their fields with, and the stone rubbers and saucer querns between which they ground their corn, their tools of flint and the pots they made. These 'Windmill Hill' people have been described not only as the first farmers in Britain but as the first industrialists. Elsewhere, for instance at Grime's Graves in Norfolk, or on the far side of Salisbury Plain around Easton Down (which is about five and a half miles out of Salisbury on the north side of the Andover road before it forks at Lopscombe Corner), they sank shafts to mine flint for their tools and weapons. And they buried their dead in the long barrows of which there are so many in Wessex.

There is a fair gap between Windmill Hill and Avebury. After these first stone-using farmers, after some five or six hundred years (about as long, that is, as the time separating us from Henry VIII or Henry VI), bronze-using peoples began to enter the country – now distinguished as the 'Beaker folk' from the drinking cups which were buried with them. They swamped and absorbed their predecessors over most of the country; and it is to these Beaker folk, cattle, sheep and pig breeders rather than tillers of the soil, that Stonehenge and Avebury, so

Dorset cliffs are bizarrely coloured – white, grey, black, yellow. Here are the golden cliffs of West Bay formed of sand separated by lines of sandstone.

Shaping stone for a London building in one of the quarries of the Isle of Portland. Wren used Portland stone for St Paul's.

4004 B.C.; and it was fabricated mainly by William Stukeley, the eighteenth-century antiquary who made – most virtuously – the first accurate survey of the two circles. If his surveys were accurate, his later notions were queer. He convinced himself that the Druids, far from being Celtic, were Phoenicians who came to Britain soon after the Flood, built our stone circles, and practised and preserved in them a pure, primitive religion which was the forerunner of Christianity. He had his reasons for all this, and they are admirably explained in *William Stukeley – An Eighteenth-Century Antiquary*, written lately by Professor Stuart Piggott, who is one of the archaeologists responsible for the modern exploration and understanding of Avebury. The fact is that both the great monuments were standing somewhere about a thousand years before a Celt or a Celtic priest can have crossed the Channel. But the legend (like the legend of the Phoenicians coming to Cornwall for tin) takes a deal of killing.

MAIDEN CASTLE

The prehistoric sequences in Wessex or any other part of Britain

Another ancient Dorset industry is making tackle at Bridport for most of the fisheries of the world. Warping cotton yarn for deep-sea fishing lines.

are too complex to squash into a few pages or sentences[1]. After Stonehenge, Avebury and the Beaker folk, culture followed culture. Thus barrows on the downs in Wiltshire, Dorset and Hampshire have given evidence of a surprisingly rich and complex 'Wessex culture' which was the next stage – one of chieftains with plenty of bronze weapons, necklaces of Baltic amber, Irish gold, Cornish tin, blue beads from the Mediterranean. Invaders from Brittany, they too, no doubt, made the customary landfall on the Hampshire coast, and pierced the forest up to the light, dry lands of the chalk. For early man Salisbury Plain was not only forest-free and suitable for field or flock: it was the heart of Britain, because men could pass easily from the Plain west and east and north on to other areas of light uplands unencumbered by a thickness of oaks. For instance, a map quickly proves how easy it must have been to travel up by the chalk past Newmarket into East Anglia and the Breckland country around Grime's Graves. The phases go on: Wessex in season, like other districts, becomes Celticized, Romanized,

1. The best available outline is Professor Stuart Piggott's *British Prehistory* (1949) in The Home University Library.

Two Dorset oddities. Chesil Bank, the long ridge of shingle stretching away to the Isle of Portland –

Anglicized and at last overrun by the Normans. Here and there other prominent sites in Wessex speak of this layer upon layer of invaders, settlers and cultures. Just outside Dorchester the immense Maiden Castle of banks and shadowed ditches deserves examination, though it is a much younger monument than Stonehenge or Avebury. The hill on which it is carved and piled was first adopted by stone-users about 2400 B.C. Some 2,000 years later, early immigrants arrived with a knowledge of iron for farming, clearing forests and fighting; they fortified the hill and lived within the ramparts. So it lasted for the best part of three centuries, under the control of successive Celtic invaders. Finally it was a stronghold of the Belgae, of mixed Celtic and German origin, who moved into Wessex in the hundred years before the Roman Conquest, entering again by way of the Dorset and Hampshire coasts. Vespasian, who afterwards became emperor, stormed Maiden Castle as commander of the 2nd Legion, probably in A.D. 43. Excavation uncovered the skeletons of the fallen Belgae; and between the vertebrae of one of the dead men lay the spearhead which killed him. Within 30 years or so the townspeople of Maiden Castle were transferred to the

- and George III on horseback cut into the chalk above Weymouth Bay. The King's holiday at Weymouth did much for its popularity as a resort.

new Roman town of Dorchester.

There is not so very much of Roman Wessex to be visited outside the museums. The best way to see how the Romans affected any part of the country is to unfold the Ordnance Survey *Map of Roman Britain.* There are the Roman roads going straight from the Roman towns of Calleva Atrebatum (Silchester), up in the sandy north-east of Hampshire, and from Venta Belgarum (Winchester); a long road cutting across Wessex from Silchester past the modern Andover and turning south-west to Durnovaria (Dorchester), and another road striking west to east from the Roman lead mines around Charterhouse on the Mendips to Old Sarum and on to Winchester. From Winchester continuations of the road come south to two of the gateways into Britain at Clausentum (Bitterne, on the edge of Southampton) and Portus Adurni (Portchester) on the northern side of Portsmouth Harbour. And Clausentum was already a gateway out as well as in, since pigs of Roman lead have been found there. The map, too, at once reveals how villas – houses and farm estates of Romanized Britons – are thick behind Portsmouth and up through Hampshire around Winchester and Andover, and how by contrast on Salisbury Plain the small upland farming villages of the British peasants persisted. There were villas too on the Isle of Wight; and in the New Forest there was a cluster of Romano-British potteries (the potters having clay, water, and wood for firing ready to hand).

A ROMAN CITY

Winchester and Dorchester are the only two Roman towns in Wessex which are towns to-day, many times their original size (unless you count Southampton as the successor of Clausentum). Outside Dorchester look at Maumbury Rings (as well as at Maiden Castle). Here, it seems, was a Bronze Age sacred site which the people of Durnovaria turned into an amphitheatre. Silchester, tucked away to the north of Basingstoke, was the little town of the kings of the Atrebates, the strongest of those Belgic tribes. In France, or rather in Gaul, their chief town had been the modern Arras, and the Atrebates who crossed over and founded Silchester left Gaul because of Julius Caesar's conquest. These Belgae were more civilized than any of the invaders before them. Their towns were the first in Britain; and Winchester, as well as Silchester, may have been a Belgic town which was then transformed by the Romans. Winchester, Dorchester and Silchester were each made by the Romans into tribal capitals. Silchester, though, was eventually deserted, perhaps because it was not the focus of a rich enough countryside. Forty or fifty years after the Roman forces abandoned Britain (in A.D. 410) it seems that town life continued there no more. But the walls remain, here and there ten or twelve feet of flint bedded in cement and stratified with courses of walling stone, the whole length of them thick with elder, ivy and tall ash trees. They enclose 104 acres of grass, as well as a farmhouse and a little medieval church side-by-side in one corner. The city wall at this point is actually the wall of the churchyard. Looking at the farmland which was once a city, you would not guess either that Silchester had been there or that it had been excavated and planned in all its details – even to recovering seeds of the plants which grew among the Roman houses and along the carefully regular streets. (The finds at Silchester are in the museum at Reading, ten miles away.)

To discover the site of Clausentum you have to cross the Itchen at Southampton by the Northam Bridge and visit the grounds of Bitterne Manor, though this is far less rewarding than a visit a few miles west to

The swanherd immobilizes one of his charges at the Abbotsbury Swannery, which is sheltered from the sea by the Chesil Bank.

Portchester. Portus Adurni sticks out into Portsmouth Harbour, pointing directly to Portsmouth itself. It stands less for the Roman heyday than for the decline of Roman Britain. The sturdy Roman walls and the 14 bastions that remain belong to one of the late forts set up under the Count of the Saxon Shore. The point of them was to protect Britain against raids by a new enemy. Portus Adurni never lost its value. In one angle there was an Augustinian priory of which the church is left. In the opposite angle are the considerable remains

(chiefly twelfth and fourteenth century) of the royal castle founded by Henry II. Here in 1415 Henry V assembled the army which was to defeat the French at Agincourt. So at Portus Adurni or Portchester (see page 36) the flood of history can be felt strongly.

For another fragment of Roman Britain, I recommend a journey out of Blandford in Dorset up the valley of the Stour. The road runs into the nobility of wood and the tall roundness of hills. Hod Hill, above Stourpaine, is covered with a large Iron Age hill-fort ditched and banked; and similar to many of the same age scattered through Wessex. Imagine the Romans on the march, in hostile country, before they settled the British to the life of town and farm estate. The Roman soldiers needed a fort for a while, or rather a defensive camp, so they cut off a small rectangle inside this vast hill-fort. Across the road from Hod Hill rises Hambledon Hill, also scarred with Iron Age banks enclosing still more space. The Dorset 'Clubmen' collected inside this fort in 1645 in defiance of Cromwell. They were countrymen sick of both sides in the Civil War. They were caught. All who did not escape by sliding down the hillside Cromwell shut up down below in Iwerne Courtney church. Both hills, Hod and Hambledon, are muffled with woods, and up Hambledon Hill climbs a black thicket of yew trees. The scene on the road between the two is one of the most delectable anywhere in Wessex.

SIXTY MILES OF WANSDYKE

Inland in the Wessex counties – certainly in Wiltshire and Dorset – the people you meet to-day, in the villages and on the farms, differ from the people farther west; and not only in their dialects, their longer, slower speech (still peppered with older words such as 'leer' for hungry). It would not be wrong, in their isolation and their scattered settlements, to call them rather more phlegmatic, rather more insular and locally minded; indeed, rather more 'English,' as if they had less mixture (as in other parts) of Celtic or Scandinavian ancestry. That our counties after the decay of the Roman power were thoroughly 'Englished' or Saxonized is clear enough, though the details are hazy. For instance, did the first Saxons, of what became Wessex historically, enter from the north, overland, or like all the previous invaders from

Opposite—The stony buildings of Dorset: (above) Houses at Swanage; (centre) The stone-walled, stone-tiled cottages at Corfe; (below) Houses down the stone-paved Gold Hill at Shaftesbury.

By order of Parliament Corfe Castle was blown up after it had succumbed to siege in the Civil War. Chunks of it lean outward over the hill. (See p. 51).

Crumpled tilted beds of Purbeck stone at Stair Hole, Lulworth Cove, which were once painted by J. M. W. Turner.

the south by way of Southampton Water or the Dorset coast? The strange earthwork of Wansdyke, running for 60 miles from Wiltshire into Somerset, may be a sign that the Romano-British had experience of raids from the north, and feared worse to come. Wansdyke is a high bank with a ditch always on the north; late Roman or probably post-Roman. For examining this mystery there are several good points. You can see it snaking up the side of All Cannings Down on the left of the road from Avebury to Devizes. A few miles east it dips and crosses the road between Alton Barnes to Lockeridge, and a stretch of it here, bank and ditch alike, is grown over with trees.

Such dykes may be late imitations of the Roman Wall. We must not imagine Wansdyke being manned by fighters for 60 miles; but a tall barrier and a deep ditch (taller and deeper than they are now) would make cattle rustling more difficult.

Whatever Wansdyke may have been, there are arguments for a northern and for a southern origin of the kingdom of the West Seaxe, the West Saxons. Charford on the east bank of the Avon below Salisbury (it is not a village and so takes a little searching for on a one-inch Ordnance map: you will find it between Downton and

Hale) may be Cerdicesford, named after the West Saxon King Cerdic, first of the line. The odd thing about Cerdic is that his name is British and not Saxon. He was the child, it is suggested, of a Saxon chief by a British mother. Cerdic's people may have crossed from the districts colonized by the Saxons on the north coasts of France; and then spread up the Avon around Salisbury. His son Cynric defeated the Britons at Old Sarum in 552, and by 556 had advanced across Wiltshire up to Beranburh, where Cynric defeated the British again. Beranburh is the modern Barbury Castle, the Iron Age earthwork on the very limit of the downs not so far from Swindon (ancient and modern fighting were bridged here across the centuries. I have seen German bombs exploding below Barbury, missing the hangars on Wroughton aerodrome. American soldiers in training dug themselves into holes within the enclosure of the camp and crouched among sherds of Iron Age pottery). From Old Sarum the Saxon settlement would thus have extended itself north into Wiltshire, east into Hampshire, west into Dorset. The early climax came when Cynric's son Ceawlin defeated the British decisively at Deorham (which is probably Dyrham, outside the region of this book, near Bath) in A.D. 577. Certainly the British upland villages of the chalk decayed. Certainly these new agricultural invaders settled along the richer lowland of the river valleys, giving Wessex the villages and the village names which persist to this day. The contrast is visible in many places. Thus north of Salisbury, left and right above the Avon, air photographs have shown the square fields of the nameless British villages (you can detect them often enough in the evening sunlight). The Saxon villages are strung through the river meadows down below, Enford (Enedford, the 'ford of ducks'), Fittleton ('Fitela's farm'), Figheldean ('Fygla's valley'), Durrington ('Deora's farm'), and so on. Bit by bit the remnants of the British probably intermixed with the newcomers and deserted their old hill fields and homes.

So the early history of Wessex has gone – from Neolithic farmers, Beaker folk building the stone temples, men of the Wessex culture, the Iron Age Celts and the Belgae, and the Romans to the Anglo-Saxons (who had much trouble in the end from the Danes); and then last of all came the Normans. Thus Wessex men and women have an ancestral mishmash behind them, even if they are predominantly English and even if Roman and Norman were rather invading overlords than a settlement of peoples.

The outer rim of the great chalk bowl of Wessex, the 'Hampshire Basin', crops up in the Isle of Wight. Here it forms some of the boldest chalk cliffs of England, ending in the Needles, masses of chalk too hard to be worn away.

This is not a history book, so for the development of the Anglo-Saxons from agricultural barbarity and division, for details, too, of the ups and downs of the West Saxons, you must go to such a book as R. H. Hodgkins's *History of the Anglo-Saxons* (1935), and discover there how Birinus brought Christianity from Rome to Wessex about A.D. 635 as Augustine had brought it to Canterbury and to the king of the men of Kent in 547, and how gradually Wessex became once more part of the Mediterranean civilization of Europe, and at last the premier kingdom and the mainstay of England against the Danes. Our concern is more with the effect of the West Saxons upon Wessex as it is now. Winchester became the capital (which had been at Dorchester-*on-Thames* earlier on) and its tradition and influence were such that the Norman conqueror William was doubly crowned – first in London, then in Winchester. Winchester has remained an attractive and venerable city, but geographically London was bound to win – indeed, had been winning since the Romans created it after their conquest and made it into the largest of the British towns (Roman London covered 303 acres, Roman Winchester 138, Silchester 104, and Dorchester 86), and with about 25,000 people one of the larger towns on this side of the Alps. Matters might have been different if the Straits of Dover had been as wide as the sea between Portsmouth and France, or if the Itchen up from Southampton Water had been as long, strong, deep and wide-mouthed as the Thames. Even then Winchester would have been in a corner. London is more in the centre for the outspread of roads (as later on of railways and air lines) and for the control of a unified England.

Yet centuries had to go by before this nearly ironless and quite coalless part of the country lost the drive of its natural advantages. Under the Anglo-Saxons its importance was maintained, in some ways increased. But what they have left behind in stone or in solid monument is scanty; it is less impressive than the leavings of the Neolithic farmers, the Beaker folk, the Celts and the Belgae or the Romans, though fascinating on that account. The Normans rebuilt most of their churches, big and little. But what Saxon churches were like you can discover from the parish church of Breamore on the road which goes down with the Avon from Salisbury or from the smaller Saxon church at Corhampton in the Meon Valley, south-west of Winchester. Wessex has two more complete Saxon churches, one in Wiltshire at

The 13th-century Salisbury Cathedral, seen from the River Nadder on a summer evening.

The bottom of the chalk bowl of Wessex has filled up with clay and sand, producing the sandy heaths of Dorset – this is Bloxworthy Heath –

Bradford on Avon (outside the area of this book) and one in Dorset, St Martin's, stuck on the earthen ramparts which surround Wareham (a church with twelfth-century wall paintings and, less to be expected, a stone figure stretched on the floor in Arab garments, who turns out to be Lawrence of Arabia carved by his friend Eric Kennington). Here and there a fragment of sculpture gives a notion – not, I am bound to say against exaggeration of their merits, a very elevating one – of Anglo-Saxon art. There are two flying angels in the church at Bradford on Avon, a flying angel on the outer wall of the church of Winterborne Steepleton near Dorchester, and man dancing on the shaft of a cross in the church of Codford St Peter (Wiltshire) in the cool valley of the Wylye. The famous rood on the wall of Romsey Abbey, the abbey church of Saxon founding which the Normans rebuilt, is probably post-Saxon of the twelfth century (though there is a small carved rood – a small panel of Christ crucified – which is undoubtedly Saxon, inside the abbey). The shallow reliefs of the Anglo-Saxon sculptor have neither the life nor the richness nor the moving power of the Romanesque carving of Norman times which the traveller will see in

– and the deep glades of the New Forest in Hampshire.

the tympana and fonts of several Wessex churches. Examine, for instance, the celebrated font in Winchester Cathedral, or the font in the church at East Meon, a few miles east of the Saxon churchlet at Corhampton, or the tympanum over the doorway of the solid, powerful church of Shalfleet in the Isle of Wight. No, the best memorial of the Saxons in this ancient kingdom of theirs is not in stone: it is in land, it is in Wessex itself, the siting of the farms and the villages, and in their names; and also in the dialects spoken by the people who live in farm and village. Breamore church by the Avon, Corhampton church by the Meon, Codford St Peter by the Wylye tell not only of how Anglo-Saxon architecture or art developed, but of how the heathen settlement began in the more fertile valleys. The wooden barns with slopes of thatch on either side, of which plenty still exist and which were still going up until the last century, may give us an idea, in a medievalized form, of how Anglo-Saxon houses looked inside the stockade of a *tun* or farm settlement. And I wonder if the Wessex habit which persisted until recently of planting yew trees alongside farmhouses and cottages is not a relic of Germanic tree worship and the importance of a guardian tree.

There are maps which present the older story of Wessex graphically and immediately – the Roman map I have mentioned, or the Ordnance map of *Britain in the Dark Ages* which depicts Wessex as King Alfred knew it, stretching between forests north, west, east, and the coasts of the Channel. A more recent Ordnance map, first published in 1944, pictures the way in which the land is utilized, dividing it up by colours, light green for meadowland, dark green for woodland, yellow for heath and moorland, brown for arable, red for urban areas. For Wessex the colours are well-mixed. In Hampshire, above Winchester, thick brown shows the fertile farming land which overlies the chalk, and recalls the reason for the close grouping of villa after villa in Roman times. Westward into Wiltshire, this brown richness thins out into islands in a green sea of the chalk grasslands (though these have been extensively broken once more for corn). Behind Lymington, Bournemouth and Swanage the yellow of heath surrounds larger and smaller islands of wood; and large areas of red show how built up the coastal areas have become about Portsmouth, Southampton and Bournemouth. Holiday-makers' red dabs the coastal circuit of the Isle of Wight. The map suggests all the variation of scene, upland, valley, relics of forest, ploughed fields, pine and heather and birch-covered common, and ugly urbanization. It tells you that the towns (Bournemouth, Southampton and Portsmouth apart) are small, and likely to be of the kind that serve a farming community: that Wessex belongs more to farm than to industry, and remains true on the whole to its historic and prehistoric character.

But its agriculture is not the old agriculture. The curve of the chalk lands had for centuries a farming based on sheep and barley, of which the last traces may soon disappear. By day the sheep were grazed on the downs, by night they were folded on the arable land, giving it fertility. Wessex was famous for its shepherds. Three hundred years ago the Wiltshireman John Aubrey (the virtuoso who was the first writer to notice and describe the temple at Avebury) worked himself into lyricism about the downs, sheep and shepherds of his county – the turf was 'of a short sweet grasse, good for the sheep, and delightfull to the eye, and pleasant to the traveller.' And as for the shepherds 'the innocent lives here of the shepherds doe give us a resemblance of the golden age.' In the fold of the downs below the road from Devizes to Avebury stands the intricate church of Bishop's

Fishing on the Test, the most celebrated of the trout streams flowing southward from the chalk uplands of Hampshire and Wiltshire.

A notable contribution to downland dairy-farming was made by a Wessex pioneer. Under the 'Hosier system' (mentioned on page 41) the cows are milked in travelling sheds. They live out and so fertilize the thin soil of the Downs.

Sheep were formerly supreme in Wessex but nowadays it is the cow. Milk tanks assembled for the journey to London.

The superb sea-gateways sheltered by the Isle of Wight were valued by the Romans, who built Portchester (Portus Adurni), with its square of bastioned walls, at the head of Portsmouth Harbour. Here, Henry V assembled the army that was victorious at Agincourt.

Southampton has had its share of armies embarking for the Continent, but its civilian exits and entrances and its gift of a double high tide have raised it to greater eminence as the home port of the largest oceanic liners. The *Queen Mary* leaving Southampton for America.

Bournemouth, youngest of the big towns of England, exists for health and pleasure and retirement. Laid out on the sandy heaths which fill the bottom of the Hampshire Basin, its gardens extend for two miles through the town. (See p. 55 and the Gazetteer.)

The waters between Southampton and the Isle of Wight are unrivalled for yachting and every fine day from spring to autumn they are white with sails. To their shores – as here at Southsea – holiday-makers crowd down from London, the Midlands and the North.

Portsmouth is the naval guardian of the Wessex sea-gateways and all that lies behind them. Part of the 'march past' on Navy Day, in front of the 18th-century dockyard offices and Nelson's *Victory*.

Cannings. The vicar of this parish, George Ferrabee, made a shepherds' entertainment for Anne of Denmark, Queen of England and wife of James I, when she was returning from Bath to London. On June 11, 1613, the Queen and her ladies left their coaches, walked over the short sweet grass up to Wansdyke on All Cannings Down and listened to the pastoral sung by the clergyman and by 'his parishioners in shepherd's weeds.' But you can drive in these days the length of the same road (and through many other stretches of upland) without seeing a sheep, or hearing, as you would have heard them even 20 years ago by Wansdyke, the sound of sheep bells. It is easier now to find the bells in Wiltshire antique shops. In Wiltshire, sheep have declined from 600,000 to about 60,000. In Dorset, 70 years back, sheep numbered 250,000. They went down to 138,000 in 1940 and to 46,000 in 1949. As one would expect, Wessex evolved several famous breeds, the older Wiltshire Horned Sheep and Dorset Horns, and especially the Hampshire Down, 'the model of a thick-fleshed sheep,' which we have to-day. If the sheep go on disappearing so fast, within less than a lifetime there will not be a plump Hampshire Down or a breeding pen of hurdles cosily stuffed with straw from one end of Wessex to the other.

The sheep are being supplanted. Nowadays the dominant animal of Wessex farming is the honest but less Arcadian cow producing gallons of milk by the million for the great cities; and milk of a steadily improving cleanliness and richness. In Hampshire, for instance, the cattle have more than doubled since 1882. If the vales are better for milk, the downs as well make their contribution. Where Anne of Denmark listened to the song of Mr Ferrabee's shepherds, you may notice here and there one of the travelling milk bails devised by a notable Wiltshire farmer, Mr A. J. Hosier. Under the 'Hosier system' the milking machine and the shed go to the cows instead of the cows going to a shed fixed in the farmyard; and the cows drop into the light downland soil a fertility trodden into it in earlier times by the sheep. A. J. Hosier, in fact, is an inventive pioneer in a good local tradition. It was not so far away, on the borders of Wiltshire and Berkshire at his farm in Shalbourne parish which he called 'Mount Prosperous,' that Jethro Tull (1674-1741) employed the corn drill he invented; and in John Fowler (1826-1864), born at Melksham – though his work was done elsewhere – Wiltshire can claim another pioneer of mechanized farming: Fowler invented ploughing by steam.

Machines of every kind in fact now do for the Wessex farmer what was done on small plots by his Neolithic predecessor with the digging stick and the hoe. On the downs, tractor and combine drill (which delivers the seed and fertilizer together) and combine harvester deal with a great acreage of wheat and barley. Drive along the road from Ludgershall to Devizes and look south across Salisbury Plain, and you will see, not without admiration, how the wide extents of wheat and barley rise and fall and curve away to the horizon. Your view will be disturbed only by an aerodrome or by army hutments, since the Services in this nasty world appropriate about a seventh of the arable lands of Wiltshire, much of it on the downs.

Local men remember their childhood and the sheep bells. They shake their heads; and they might quote, if they knew them, lines written about those business-like monks who owned so much of Wessex and worked the wool trade so skilfully :

The sward the blackface browses,
The stapler and the bale,
The grey Cistercian houses
That pack the wool for sale.

You and he and I may prefer to look at downs with sheep, but we are in the middle rather of an agricultural revolution, helped on by the war, than of an agricultural disaster. Great Britain has needed milk and grain. Throughout Wessex the stimulus and difficulties of the times have made the farmer produce thousands of extra tons of food, and extra gallons of milk, every season. If he has done it, here as elsewhere in Wessex and in Great Britain, if he has replaced horses with tractors and has steadily been replacing sheep with his red or white speckled Shorthorns, feeding them on the grass leys which in turn are ploughed for the barley and the wheat, we can only admit that farming like everything else has to change.

Still it is true that the decline of sheep is also likely to change the scenery of the downs. John Aubrey wrote not only of the short grass smooth as a bowling green but of areas (such as persist in Cranborne Chase) of particular pleasantness where the downs 'are intermixt with boscages.' This mixture of grass and boscage, clear and scrub, lawn in the old sense of the word and cover, must have been more or less general when the downs were inhabited by the Bronze Age shepherding peoples; the sheep increase, and nibble, and the boscage

Portsmouth's naval tradition: figureheads of old men-of-war in the H.M.S. Victory Museum.

decreases, and the smooth bowling greens widen and produce that other kind of delightful scenery we know. Remove the sheep and the process is reversed, boscage increases, the scrub will spread, and dark juniper, snowy may trees and dogwood and wayfaring tree will muffle the ancient smoothness. Unless the old methods and practices are continued deliberately here and there, and sheep are, so to say, artificially preserved (there are scientists who urge the doing of this within limits), then our great-grandchildren will find the downs different altogether. Much of Wessex will display a face it has not worn for some four or five thousand years and generations ahead may have to push their way to Stonehenge through the scrub.

Neither downland nor downland vale farming are the whole of Wessex agriculture. The soils are too mixed despite the preponderance of chalk, especially in Dorset. Where there is sand, though not too much of it, there is mixed farming; where there is clay (as in parts of Dorset north-west of Blandford or in much of Hampshire, though Hampshire has the thickest concentration of land which is used for crops) you will find grass and cows. The big population of Bournemouth, Southampton and Portsmouth makes market-gardening worth while within reach of them, where the soil allows it. Botley, between Southampton and Portsmouth, has a name for strawberries. If you go into East Hampshire around Alton, towards the border of Surrey, parts of the country are measured out with hop poles, as though it were Herefordshire or Kent; and I am not sure that a hillside with hops is not more attractive formally than a vineyard in Southern France or along the Rhine. The growing of watercress is another matter. It is one of the minor industries of our time in Hampshire (and in Wiltshire) without much charm. The gently falling valleys of Hampshire and Wiltshire streams lend themselves to it, and the ponds and races of derelict watermills can be adapted easily enough for watercress beds, which are insipid and unlovely objects as one can see quickly enough in Eastern Hampshire at Alresford and Basing. Still, watercress is not grown on a scale great enough to interfere with the general delights of the eye.

Generally it is true to say that the scenery of Wessex is man-made and that the man who made it through the centuries has been the estate-owner and the farmer. If it is our fashion to prefer wild to tame (and it was a Wessex author, Thomas Hardy, who foretold that 'the chastened sublimity of a moor, a sea or a mountain' would be 'all of nature that is absolutely in keeping with the moods of the more thinking among mankind'), wilderness is not everything. True the wild breaks out, or at least the semi-wild breaks out among the tamed landscape of Wessex, but there are moods nevertheless when one prefers the comfort and homeliness of a countryside in which man has always been at home.

An old mine from which stone was raised in the Isle of Purbeck.

TWO CATHEDRALS

In the modern Great Britain our district is poor rather than wealthy. In earlier centuries when wealth was measured in land and its produce, there was wealth enough for the people of Wessex to ornament the landscape with good architecture, particularly in the valleys and the towns into which the agricultural wealth flowed and collected. The two great buildings are the cathedrals of Winchester and Salisbury. They could hardly be more unlike, Winchester long and low, Salisbury compact and aspiring; Winchester a complex of periods mixing the severity of Romanesque (as in the north wing of the transept) with the lighter work of the fourteenth and fifteenth centuries in the nave, Salisbury an intricate composition of one period (1220-1260), delicate, unified, netted with slender piers and pointed arches, a purity of Gothic – with an English accent. Like Stonehenge and Avebury, Salisbury Cathedral is one of the principal structures of Great Britain, admirably fitted to the width and flatness of its situation; and the city around it is alive and active and large enough to balance the cathedral in its green close.

Considering how much of Wessex was held by the church in the Middle Ages, and how many religious houses there were, Wessex has been unfortunate in losing much of its monastic architecture, Salisbury and Winchester apart. In Dorset it would not do to miss the Romanesque work of Wimborne Minster, or the abbey church with its superbly fresh, yellow and white interior in the park at Milton Abbas, or the Perpendicular richness of the abbey church at Sherborne, or in Hampshire the Romanesque of the monastic churches at Romsey and Christchurch. In Wiltshire, Edington has a church large and sumptuous enough for a cathedral – all that is left of an Augustinian house of the Order of Bonhommes. It was raised by William of Edington, the bishop who began the building of the nave of Winchester Cathedral. For the rest there are either ruins or remnants or transformations. The monastic tithe barn at Abbotsbury and the gatehouse of the Benedictine Abbey of Cerne are tantalizing fragments of a lost architecture (though Cerne Abbas is more notable for itself and for the Cerne Giant, carved into the chalk slopes of Giant Hill above the site of the abbey, an unabashed monstrosity believed now to be a Romano-British figure of a Hercules cult, though one may ask why the Benedictine monks allowed it to remain)[1]. The excavated scraps of the great abbey at Shaftesbury are only one reason for visiting, on its ridge over a wide landscape, one of the most unusually situated towns in Wessex. The more elaborate ruins of Netley and Beaulieu Abbeys near Southampton are both greenly and exquisitely placed, and there is a charm of situation about the few pieces of Quarr Abbey in the Isle of Wight above the Solent.

Wessex churches cannot be characterized in a formula, gaunt little buildings on the downs, buildings more elaborate in the vales and valleys, flint churches, small timber churches or churches with timber bellcotes in Hampshire, flint churches again in Dorset, and off the chalk especially towards Somerset, tall-towered stone churches. The Romanesque church I find most moving (the Saxon churches have been mentioned already) is the minute Dorset church at Studland. No more than nave and chancel, it is like a cave or a hermitage let into a tidy church-

1. The Wiltshire white horses and the mounted horse cut into the chalk at Osmington in Dorset are all modern, inspired by antiquarian interest during the eighteenth century in the Iron Age horse at Uffington, on the edge of the Berkshire Downs. Some of the dates are Westbury, 1778, Cherhill, 1789, Alton Barnes (above the Vale of Pewsey), 1812, Osmington, 1815, Hackpen, 1838. New Zealand troops cut the kiwi on Beacons Hill at Bulford, Salisbury Plain, in 1918. Australian troops of the First World War cut a rising sun, a map of Australia, and a kangaroo alongside various English regimental badges into Forant Down on the left of the main road from Salisbury to Shaftesbury.

yard. Winchester Cathedral or the great Romanesque minsters have a cold impersonality; Studland has an intimate personality suggesting, as intensely as Durham Cathedral or St Bartholomew the Great in London, an ancient, powerful and somewhat demon-haunted form of Christianity.

One thing all the counties and the Isle of Wight possess is a plenitude of elaborate monuments to wealthy proprietors of the sixteenth, seventeenth and eighteenth centuries. A little east of Salisbury there is a fine assembly of baroque memorials in the old church (now disused) of West Dean. Farley, a few miles away, gave rise to the family of the Earls of Ilchester. Sir Stephen Fox employed Sir Christopher Wren's master-mason to build him a red brick group of church and alms-houses, of which the vicar of the parish is the warden. The Foxes are concentrated here with monuments and tablets of some elaboration. Neither English nor Latin were suitable for commemorating Sir Stephen and his wife: between classical pillars and under cherubs' heads, the inscription on their memorial is in French, beginning with the old formula 'Cy gist' and ending 'Dieu aye Merci de leurs Ames' as if they had died in the days of the Norman dynasty instead of in the eighteenth century. The greatest of the family, the statesman Charles James Fox (1749-1806), is treated rather scurvily to the smallest memorial. The Worsley memorials in Godshill church in the Isle of Wight give an intricate splendour to an interior also containing a medieval wall-painting of Christ crucified on a lily (or is it more prosaically a budding tree?).

The Dorset church of Wimborne St Giles is splendidly furnished with memorials to the Earls of Shaftesbury. Here the memorials are in a notable eighteenth-century church and it was the fashion earlier to dislike post-Reformation churches as much as post-Reformation memorials and sculpture. The distaste still lingers. For all that, look as well into the humbler eighteenth-century village churches (both in Hampshire) of Wolverton near Kingsclere and Avington in the Itchen Valley. Avington has been left alone; Wolverton has been piously modified. In Avington traditional oak is replaced with the Georgian and exotic elegance of mahogany, which a nineteenth-century parson would have felt to be more in keeping with his port and madeira than with his collects and prayers. And have your revenge on the century which first scorned these classical churches, by trying a few minutes in St Mildred's at Whippingham in the Isle of Wight, an architectural monster designed by the Prince Consort and built by Queen Victoria, which is full of regal fittings and royal needlework. Queen Victoria's Osborne House is nearby. The official guide to Osborne (which is open three days a week) says a little evasively that it was 'designed in the Palladian style, more for comfort than for architectural effect.' It is the most curious assembly (though the Russel-Cotes Art Gallery at Bournemouth runs it close) of the very centre of Victorian taste in the arts – pictures by Winterhalter and by landscape painters of the Düsseldorf school, a billiard table with ornamentation after Raphael, a waste-paper basket in fancy cane, bric-à-brac of every kind, and a bronze statuette of the Prince Consort in Highland dress, with a collie. In the Swiss Cottage are the gardening tools used in the 'fifties by the royal children.

PRIVATE PALACES

Great houses elsewhere in Wessex are rather more satisfying to the spirit. There are plenty of them, from the grey-towered Longford Castle of the sixteenth century in the Avon valley at Britford near Salisbury, to the long, low exquisiteness of Forde Abbey in Dorset – far Dorset on the Somerset border – a blending of medieval tit-bits with the classical innovations of Inigo Jones and his pupil, John Webb. West of Salisbury, Wiltshire has the finest group of all – Wilton, to begin with, the palace of the Earls of Pembroke, where Inigo Jones and Webb again were at work in the seventeenth century; then the classical mansion of Wardour Castle (1770-1776), with the ruins of the old fourteenth-century castle a few minutes away, decked with fine timber and a neo-Gothic garden house; then Stourhead and Longleat. One house is missing. North-west of Wardour Castle, the maligned millionaire genius William Beckford, or rather his architect, James Wyatt, raised the neo-Gothic 'abbey' of Fonthill near the source of the Nadder. Well may we regret that Wyatt built this palace with too little skill, and that the lofty tower which rose above it fell in 1825, never (like the rest of the abbey) to be rebuilt. Extravagant Fonthill must have been, but if it had survived it would be one of the chief architectural fantasias of European romanticism. Hardly a stone is left; so after finding the artificial caves which Beckford contrived down by the lake, and which are a brilliant conceit, one can travel on to the classicism, the Palladianism, against which the romantic Beckford revolted, at Stourhead.

Stourhead belongs now to the National Trust, and is a banker's

The cyclopean gateway into the Kitchen Court of Eastbury House, Dorset. Built by Sir John Vanbrugh and like a ruin in the jungles of Yucatan: see following pages.

princely combination of architecture and pleasure ground. First, a Palladian mansion with its pillars and pediment, then pleasure grounds, contrived later, with lakes, a Pantheon, a Temple of Flora, a Temple of the Sun, and a grotto through which the water of the infant Stour comes out beneath the grotto's reclining genius – a nymph carved in lead by Rysbrack. In all, eighteenth-century England created in Stourhead one of its best works of art. The earlier mansion and the park of Longleat, farther north within the triangle formed by Frome, Warminster and Maiden Bradley, are excellent, but less peculiar. Wessex is short of another huge mansion, at Eastbury Park, a mile or two north of the road out from Blandford towards Salisbury. Here Vanbrugh, whose architecture was solid, cyclopean, in an eighteenth-century way, and disturbingly imaginative, built a palace for Bubb Dodington. It must have spoken in a loud though modulated voice in the manner of his famous buildings at Blenheim and at Seaton Delaval in Northumberland. Eastbury was finished in 1738 and pulled down, most of it, before it had been standing a century, though Vanbrugh's architecture would last, one might think, as long as Stonehenge. There is a wing left, but more indicative of the scale of Vanbrugh's strange thinking is an enormous archway into the Kitchen Court, with pine trees growing out of its masonry. It looks, in this English park, rather as if one of the buildings of Chichen-Itza has been transferred from the jungles of Yucatan.

The National Trust owns nothing else in the area covered by this book so magnificent as Stourhead, though its properties include Dinton House in the Nadder valley, between Wilton and Fonthill, a neo-Grecian mansion built by James Wyatt's nephew, Sir Jeffrey Wyatville, and in the same parish the cottage once occupied by William Lawes, the seventeenth-century composer, and the stone-tiled farmhouse of Little Clarendon. In the Isle of Purbeck the Trust has a more peculiar object under its care, the folly of Grange Arch, on the high point of Ridgeway Hill, which is worth climbing to for itself and for the superlative vista of sea and Poole Harbour and the surface of Purbeck. It was set up in the eighteenth century by one of the Bonds living below in Creech Grange, another of whose family gave the name to Bond Street in London. In Dorset, too, the Trust preserves the isolated cottage at Higher Bockhampton, off the main road between Dorchester and Puddletown, in which Thomas Hardy was born, almost in the woods, in 1840. Here his mother came back up the lane to find a snake

– the story does not say whether it was an adder or a harmless grass-snake – curled on his breast as he lay in his cradle, 'comfortably asleep like himself'. Outside Stinsford Church (Higher Bockhampton is in Stinsford parish) Hardy's heart is buried under the yew tree with his two wives. There it was placed by his brother at the same moment by the clock when the Prime Minister of the day, and Housman, Kipling and Bernard Shaw, followed his ashes into Westminster Abbey.

In northern Hampshire, a few yards from Highclere Station, another National Trust property is the Oratory of All Souls with its two attendant almshouses. It was finished in 1927, and commemorates a young soldier killed in the first world war. Outside, this brick building is a little too reminiscent of one of the earlier London tube stations. Inside, the walls are covered with paintings of the war and of war hospitals by Stanley Spencer, coming to a climax over the altar in a wall full of soldiers rising from the dead on the Salonika front and handing in the white crosses they require no longer to a small figure of Christ in the background. One could find fault with the paintings. They may seem secular and not religious, they may win a peculiarity by distortions of the figure for which there is no pictorial or emotive reason. But there is enough in them, if they last, to intrigue spectators in a century or two centuries' time.

Some of the castles I have mentioned – Portchester, and the ruins of the old castle at Wardour. There are few of them. The two most eminent otherwise are Carisbrooke Castle in the Isle of Wight, above Newport, and Corfe Castle in the Isle of Purbeck, both of them – with plenty of excuse – much sketched and photographed. Carisbrooke was first built by the Normans on a site easily defended where there had been a small Roman fort. Both have associations with the Civil War: Carisbrooke because Charles I was imprisoned there before he was decapitated, Corfe because it had to undergo a Parliamentary siege. Its moving ruination was the sequel. By order of the Parliament Corfe was savagely demilitarized with kegs of gunpowder. But it was too massive to be blown to dust or for what was left to dwindle into insignificance. Chunks sag this way and that; and there Corfe remains in its gap between the green hills above Poole Harbour, one of the most dramatic ruins and dramatically sited of all the lowland castles of Great Britain, rising from a stony village of extraordinary perfection. These are land castles. Hurst Castle belongs to the sea. As you cross from Lymington to the Isle of Wight it floats on the sea at the tip of a long shingle bar from the mainland which half closes the way into the Solent. It is a Tudor defence, one of a chain extending to the Isles of Scilly in the Atlantic; and, since it is still in military occupation, look at it is all you can do. It is worthwhile.

VILLAGES IN WESSEX

The villages through Wessex do not often quarrel with their landscape. Their thatched cottages are pretty but too often ill-equipped survivals; architecturally, in some of the villages, as humble as if they had grown up out of a potato patch. Again and again the new publicly owned houses have been added with no regard for the village as a living unit. Again and again their scale is wrong and their appearance no pleasure; but if you go into them you will find they are often better fitted than farmhouse, vicarage or manor and you will see how they make it possible for the worker to live with comfort, cleanliness and sanitation. A village may be pretty, like Wherwell in Hampshire, or the Dorset villages of Wimborne St Giles or Witchampton, yet have its drawbacks. Many of these villages have, for instance, an antique grouping due to the old organization of the manor. As well as church, vicarage or rectory, manor house, inn and cottages, a number of farmhouses and farmyards will be grouped together. When the open fields, which had been cultivated strip by strip from these yards, were enclosed and divided among the farms, the houses and the yards stayed where they had always been, with results none too convenient to the farmers or to their neighbours. The farmers in many parishes have a field here and a field there to add to their work, and if the cattle are driven into the yards to be milked the village has to suffer from dirty roads. Some of the villages have an especial fame, Steventon, for instance, where Jane Austen's father was rector, and where Miss Austen was born and bred and wrote her earlier novels (it lies west of Basingstoke in Hampshire) or Chawton just outside Alton where she wrote *Persuasion* and *Emma* and lived in a house which is still there, neither pretentious nor demure. Hambledon, not far from the Meon valley, has an appeal for English, Dominion and West Indian tastes as the village where the odd English game of cricket took shape in the eighteenth century. Here was the Hambledon Club, and here indeed is the Bat and Ball Inn. Tolpuddle on the main road from Bere Regis to Dorchester is known to Trade Unionists for grimmer recollections. The six labourers of Tolpuddle, the 'Tolpuddle Martyrs', attempted to form a union in the

Wessex churches have many fine monuments to departed landlords. The monument to Robert Pierrepoint (*c.* 1670) in the abandoned church of West Dean, Wiltshire.

bad thirties, were tried for illegal conspiracy at Dorchester in 1834, and transported. Outside the chapel where they worshipped in Tolpuddle there are tablets unveiled in 1912 by Arthur Henderson, an architect of the Labour Party and afterwards Foreign Secretary. Words spoken by one of the martyrs, George Loveless, in his own defence, are cut into the marble: 'We have injured no man's reputation, character, person, or property; we were uniting together to preserve ourselves, and our wives and our children, from utter degradation and starvation.' Later still the Trade Union Congress built six memorial cottages along the main road. In a sense the farm workers of Wessex, better paid, if not always better housed even now, owe their prosperity to the six martyrs. Another Dorset village, Milton Abbas, already mentioned for the abbey church, shows the power which landlords of the eighteenth and nineteenth centuries had over their working men. The Earl of Dorchester bought the Abbey, and had no liking for a village or villagers around the church or his mansion. So in 1786 the villagers were moved to the new model village of thatched houses running up hill above the park the Earl had contrived. It was no doubt a good exchange, which could be called despotism tempered with benevolence; and we may now enjoy the look of the houses, pair and pair, divided by horse-chestnuts and verged with grass.

For a less-known contrast in the behaviour of landlords, go to the Dorset parishes of Corscombe and Halstock near the edge of Somerset below Yeovil. Here the landlord was the eccentric Thomas Hollis, passionate about the promotion, celebration and preservation of liberty. He gave books to Harvard as a university of the free, and he renamed his farms and the fields on them after regicides, tyrannicides, champions of freedom, republicans and philosophers. All the names are still in use – such as Harvard Farm, Milton and Marvell Farms after the poets, Locke Farm after the philosopher. On Harvard and Marvell Farms, which go together, the fields include New England, Boston, Massachusetts, as well as Mayhew, Cotton, Eliot and Adams for whom an English, but not an American, reader will have to turn to an encyclopaedia. A farmer may put his cows in Confucius or Plato, Toleration or Magna Charta, Luther or Peters (after Hugh Peters, the chaplain at the execution of Charles I). Hollis himself, reviled as a 'democratical' man or madman, fell dead on his estates on New Year's Day in 1774 and by his own order was buried ten feet down on Urles Farm in Corscombe, without a monument.

BLANDFORD FORUM

Inland, our district has no big towns and nothing to call them into being. Winchester and Salisbury are unique as centres of good building, dignity, tradition and fair size. Dorchester, Dorset's county capital, is little more, clean and pleasant as it may be, than a small market town, rather gently asleep. There is hardly an inland town, Hungerford, Newbury, Alton, Petersfield, Basingstoke, Romsey, Warminster, Shaftesbury, Mere, Wimborne, Marlborough, Devizes, Sherborne, without something to show in the way of dignified domestic building; but of all the towns, inland or along the coast, there is none with such an architectural unity and dignity as Blandford. Blandford was lucky in two accidents: most of it was burnt in 1731, and when it came to rebuilding there were two local architects, John and William Bastard. They gave this previously unremarkable place a classical rebirth. They raised it into cousinship at least with eighteenth-century Bath. Bath, though, is a planned city; Blandford a country town with lovely brick buildings set out upon its old intricacy. The eighteenth-century face of Blandford – Blandford Forum since the rebirth – has weathered and worn into a certain shabbiness, as if this once smart dress was now a little too much for it. Perhaps the dress was too sophisticated for its real marketing status. But then Bath as well has lost some of its elegant self-confidence, and the shabbiness of Blandford's flowered coat and wig is not ill-becoming.

The inland towns are the natural urban concentrations of an agricultural district with few industries; the coast towns, on the Hampshire coast, have had their chance to swell. First of all, to say it once more, Southampton and Portsmouth (both severely visited by German bombers) were gateways to a hinterland. Southampton now is the civilian, Portsmouth the military, or rather the naval, protector. From either it is an easy, quick journey to London. They enjoy shelter, deep water runs up to Southampton Docks, and Southampton has the gift of a double high tide, two periods of high water with a couple of hours between them. So it is a town of exits and entrances, particularly for passengers, across to the Continent, to the Americas and South Africa, the town of the great liners and all the emotion of meeting and parting; and, though it has risen to its passenger eminence within the last hundred years and has acquired industries, it is still an old town, going back to the Roman Clausentum, to importance under the Saxons, under the Normans, and through the Middle Ages, with architectural remains (in spite of bombing) to tell something of its past. The greater swelling of Bournemouth, Boscombe, Branksome, Parkstone into one huge aggregate farther west across heaths which were useless and forbidding, has to do with pleasure, good air, and long sands rather than with vulgar uses. The pine trees and the warmth and shelter of Poole Bay were thought to be good for Victorian consumptives. The railway came and Bournemouth grew. The single villa of 1810 became a town of nearly 2,000 people within 50 years. By 1890 the two thousand had multiplied by ten. Bournemouth has increased like water spreading from a spilt bucket till the twenty thousand has been multiplied nearly by seven. Trains come quickly down from the North through Somerset, and quickly from London, and the trains have been outsmarted by the car and the motor-coach until Bournemouth has become much more than a place for the sick, the retired or the middle-class family on holiday. Bournemouth is the youngest of the big towns of England; and young towns without a heart are seldom satisfying or beautiful, even if they have no factory chimneys and are placed on the edge of Poole Bay and among pine trees and rhododendrons.

THE QUARRY COAST

If saved is the right word, the Dorset coast has been saved by tall cliffs and a more open coast, by communications which are far less convenient, and by the sudden division of the countryside due to the inland bulge of Poole Harbour. Eastward from Bournemouth the coast belongs to the pleasure-orbit of London – Bournemouth, Milford, Ventnor, Sandown, Hayling Island, Bognor, Littlehampton, Worthing, Hove, Brighton, Eastbourne and so on round to Folkestone and Margate. The whole of Hampshire, indeed, except for parts of the downland country and the New Forest, has a tinge of London and the metropolitan about it, which extends into the Isle of Wight in spite of its seventeenth-century manor-houses and Early Victorian villas. It is in Wiltshire with no sea-coast, and Dorset with the most peculiar of coasts from the Isle of Purbeck to Lyme Regis, that the visitor or the native begins to be delivered from the pressure of his companions. Not that the Dorset coast – Studland, Swanage, Weymouth, Charmouth and Lyme – is unfrequented. But the sea towns – even Weymouth – have not been too much transformed. They keep the character of a slow growth from an ancient childhood (Lyme Regis is architecturally the most delightful of them), and they are separated one from another by stretches of strange-featured coast, far superior to the low, if here and there attractively wooded, shores of Hampshire. In fact the intricate geology of southern Dorset does the trick, the cliffs of chalk and Purbeck and Portland

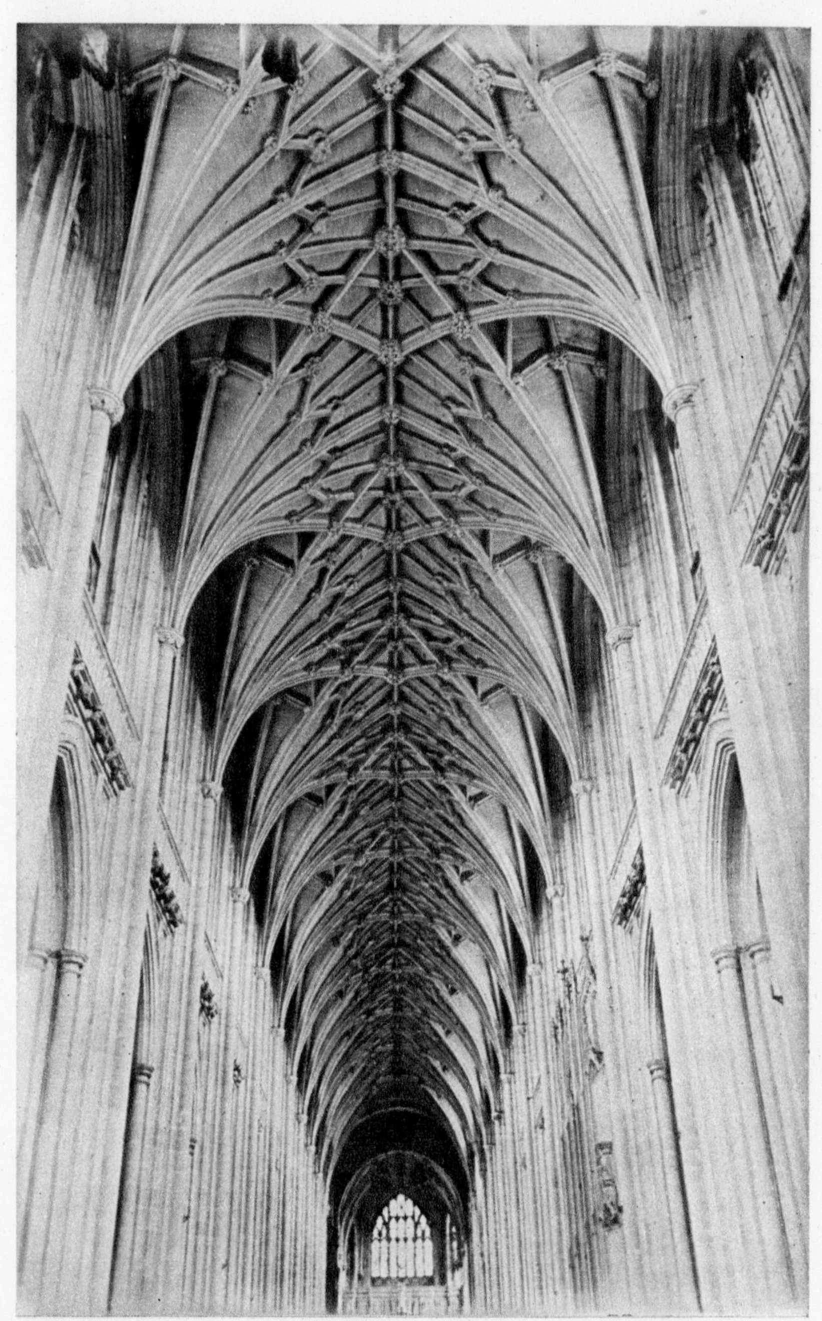

Winchester Cathedral: the vaulting of the nave (early 15th century).

stones, of shale, and of clay, and the 18 long miles of the grinding pebbles of the Chesil Bank running along as though a stony Wansdyke had been set up against the sea from the Isle of Portland past Fleet (the chief scene of one of the best of all Wessex adventure stories, *Moonfleet*, by Meade Falkner) to Abbotsbury, where it protects the celebrated and still flourishing swannery. There are not sandy beaches enough on the broken line of the Dorset coast for a steady extension of the pleasure strip. It is a line full of the unexpected, the old workings of the Tilly Whim caves, the length of shale coming up to the magnificence of Gad Cliff where in warm weather the oil in the cliff can be *smelt*, the vertical cliffs and the quarries of the Isle of Portland, a grey world stuck out into the Channel on its own, and the clayey cliffs around Lyme Regis, which were haunted rather more than a century ago by the 'eminent female fossilist', the self-taught Mary Anning of Lyme, who splashed and squelched about in her pattens under the cliffs, with a small dog at her feet, and discovered the first ichthyosaurus, plesiosaurus and pterodactyl. There is a window to her, and she well deserves it, in Lyme church. Yet there is irony in this window, since Mary Anning's discoveries did much to upset religious fundamentalism.

Dorset is a county with a very sharp spice of the exceptional – curious, quickly changing scenery, this curious coast, and a sense of being cut away from the rest of southern or western England. Into the bargain the county has produced curious people such as Mary Anning, or Thomas Hollis, or General Pitt-Rivers, Fellow of the Royal Society, princely archaeologist, and founder of the museum I have mentioned down a country lane near the Dorset Farnham, which he filled with the fruits of excavation, and with bronzes from Benin and statuettes from Easter Island. Curious, too, is apt enough on a higher level for the Dorset writers, Thomas Hardy and his master in poetry, William Barnes, who wrote in dialect some of the most sophisticatedly simple of all English lyrics (which anyone can get the hang of, dialect or no, in five minutes). The quarries of Dorset are simply part of the exceptional, and they repay examination, open quarries in Portland and now for the most part in Purbeck, where only two of the old underground quarries are still worked. It was in Purbeck that the black marble of medieval church architecture was raised and sent as far afield as Durham and Normandy. Purbeck men quarried it, cut it into thin shafts and polished it, or carved it on the spot into effigies. The heyday of the marble industry was between the twelfth and fourteenth centuries; and slender shafts of Purbeck marble are united with the piers in the cathedral at Salisbury. A little marble is still raised with the help of bulldozers to shift the overburden. The small surface quarries of Purbeck stone flourish; though, ignominiously perhaps, the stone is chiefly cut now into crazy paving, bird baths and rather banal ornaments for the garden and into kerb stones for Bournemouth and Southampton. The quarries are mostly small family concerns, scarcely mechanized. In the Isle of Portland, though the quarrymen form a community as close and individualized, machinery is used so far as it can be in the quarrying of the freestone, and the quarries are owned by companies. Since Inigo Jones used Portland stone for the Banqueting Hall in Whitehall, which was built between 1619 and 1622, and since Wren used it for his churches and St Paul's after the Fire, a vast bulk has been transported to London, by rail (which comes into the island) instead of by sea as in Wren's day. And Portland stone is going over the Atlantic now for the United Nations building.

PECULIAR INDUSTRIES

The explanation of the quarries and the tougher cliffs of the Dorset coast is that the older limestones crop up from beneath the younger chalk which dominates Wessex and forms the Hampshire Basin. If the quarry workings and the tip-heaps either in Purbeck or Portland are bare and uncomfortably gaunt on a dull day, both these districts of ancient closed communities with their own customs and survivals are fascinating to anyone who has not a conventional view of the picturesque. Apart from working the land, working the stone is the oldest and most enduring of the Wessex industries; and stone is not the only substance which has been exploited in this geological museum. Kimmeridge shale has been dug for marling the land. The dark brown bituminous stone known as 'Kimmeridge Coal' has been mined along the sea ledges below Kimmeridge and made into cups and bowls and ornaments as far back as Roman and prehistoric times. The clays, for instance behind the Chesil Bank, are made into bricks and tiles; shale oil has been extracted – with little profit – around Kimmeridge, and deep borings after oil were made, unsuccessfully, on the headland of Broad Bench above Hobarrow Bay in the late thirties, at Ringstead farther along the coast towards Weymouth, and behind Ringstead at Poxwell and Sutton Poyntz. In the Isle of Purbeck, if you stand on the hill by Grange Arch (p. 50), or on the jutting hill of Corfe Castle, you can look northward over the heaths where the Dorset ball-clays are mined, valuable pure clays carried here by an ancient river and formed of the decomposed granite of Devonshire. In older days the clay was dug out of open pits, much as the china clay is dug around St Austell in Cornwall. The pits have filled up into pools of blue water, which add colour to the heath. Gravel and sand in these days of concrete are another valuable commodity of Wessex, for which one has to thank the bowl of chalk – or perhaps curse it, for the pits give you in the summer what has been called 'an illusion of the Libyan desert'. The place to experience this illusion is on the heaths – Thomas Hardy's 'Egdon' – east of Dorchester between Warmwell and the railway to the north of it. Eastward again, in the Southampton and Portsmouth neighbourhood, there is a clash of interests between the farmers (and the preservers) and the gravel extractors. Here the gravel has to come out of 'wet pits' which fill up into lagoons. In the Avon Valley also, by a recent decision, a good many acres of land are to be turned into wet desert in this way.

Other industries through time have been spotted about the countryside and the coast, dependent for the most part on local accidents of terrain and people. The prosperity of Lymington, for instance, used to depend on the 'salterns', the salt pans of considerable antiquity outside the town on the low edge of the Solent; and across the water salt was dried out on the Isle of Wight. Silk, since there were refugees from France to make a beginning, was woven at Winchester, Andover, Alton, Whitchurch, Odiham and elsewhere; and lace was made at Blandford, Sherborne and Lyme Regis. A few industries from the past go on locally in this small way, such as making rope and nets at Bridport in Dorset, or paper at Laverstoke in the valley of the Test, where the mill has been producing the paper for Bank of England notes for more than two hundred years. Wilton, too, still weaves its carpets. But it is only the areas around Portsmouth and Southampton that have population enough to attract and develop new industries of one kind and another (or expand old ones) and so add them to the dockyards. The old Southampton was too far from the coal mines; the new Southampton can supply her factories with electric power. Southampton is not dependent alone on passengers, exports or imports. The factories have increased, making many things from yachts to aeroplanes, electric cables to margarine. Eastleigh, another Swindon on a small scale, building rolling-stock for the railways, is practically a suburb of Southampton; and of the new enterprises the largest and most essential is the huge oil

Crichel House, Dorset, one of many 18th-century mansions in Wessex.

refinery now busy at Fawley on the west side of Southampton Water, which has helped to take petrol off the ration and to ease Great Britain's dollar difficulties with America.

The spread of these Hampshire towns, the adding of street to street, the mixture of the mass holiday life and the mass working life – all these provoke that uneasy Hampshire feeling that London is only just out of sight beyond the chalk hills, and that Hampshire will soon have to be numbered among the Home Counties. Yachts on the Solent, or the sight of an ocean liner moving outward through this width of sheltered sea on a sparkling day, may change one's mood and make one think such feelings a parochial selfishness. Here on the magnificent scale, after all, is the ancient Exit and Entrance; but here a new character is being formed and the nagging transition is expressed not only in modern factories or a modern oil-refinery, but in a seaside shack or a rusty tin shed on an allotment, or in the indestructible rubbish men leave behind them either as industrialists or makers of war. Portsmouth is a different town from the one which saw the birth of Charles Dickens, or of the valet and naval outfitter's son, George Meredith; the Isle of Wight, though farming goes on and the islanders talk of the mainland people as 'overners', has become another island – with rural tea-gardens, crowded beaches and holiday-camps – from the one Tennyson knew in retreat at Farringford, and in which Swinburne was buried in the new graveyard at Bonchurch. The changes mix the good and the less good.

BUTTERFLIES, BIRDS AND PLANTS

No district more suggests the need for that planned preservation of scenery and wild life to which so much thought has been given in Great Britain in the last few years. North of Portsmouth the proposed National Park of the South Downs will thrust a salient over the Hampshire border, taking in Butser Hill and the hills towards the Meon and going as far north as the hanger country around Selborne, the home of Gilbert White (1720–1793), one of the best writers of Wessex as well as one of the greatest of English naturalists. Much of the Dorset Downs, heaths and coast, of Cranborne Chase and the West Wiltshire Downs, the Marlborough and the Berkshire Downs, the Hampshire Downs and the New Forest and the south-western coast of the Isle of Wight from the Needles to St Catherine's Point, are to be made into 'conservation areas', so that their scenery and delights can be preserved as much as possible; and within these areas, if all goes well, there will be national nature reserves and protected geological monuments, reserves of Dorset heath along Poole Harbour and by Wareham, reserves in the New Forest and the chalk country of the Meon and on the Hampshire coast by Hurst Castle. The geological monuments required – all are worth seeing – are the Fossil Forest of ancient trees half-way down the cliff between Lulworth Cove and Mupe Bay, to the east; to the west the natural archway of Durdle Door, a wall of Portland stone sticking out fantastically into the sea; the toad-like Agglestone, the lump of hard sandstone protecting a small hill on the brown heath behind Studland; and up north the Wiltshire sarsen stones on Fyfield Down above Avebury.

For the naturalist there is a great diversity, but no one part so rich as the New Forest for birds and mammals, insects and plants. In the New Forest there are red deer, descendants of those deer held to have been established in the glades by William the Conquerer who 'loved tall stags as if he were their father', and in the plantations here of the Forestry Commission there are fallow deer, roe deer and Japanese deer, three introduced species. In the Forest (and in the Isle of Wight as well) lives the rarest of English bats, Bechstein's Bat, common enough abroad, but in Hampshire an invader at the limit of his range who has never pierced as far inland as the Neolithic or the Anglo-Saxon farmer. But among the branches you are more likely to be pleased (since one bat to the common eye looks like another) by the sight of the red squirrel, here not entirely displaced by the woodland rat – the coarser grey squirrel introduced so unluckily from North America. As for birds, the New Forest and its fringes have as mixed a population as you can find in Southern England, including nightingale, blackcap and garden-warbler; which was why Sir Edward Grey brought Theodore Roosevelt here on a famous walk to hear English song-birds. There is a variety of habitats in the Forest, woodland and bog and wet heath, so a good many less common and more local species are present – Dartford Warbler and red-backed shrike, buzzard, hobby, wood-lark, and now and then Montagu's Harrier; there are nesting records even of the honey-buzzard. Besides an admirable frequency of rare plants (the species include the lungwort whose blue spring flowers are more familiar in the garden) the New Forest has its plethora of butterflies (and entomologists in pursuit of them) – such as the White Admiral, the Silver-studded Blue, the Silver-washed Fritillary and the Purple Emperor.

Coastal Dorset and Hampshire and the Isle of Wight owe something of their aristocracy of living creatures and plants not only to the combination of habitat, soil, structure and climate, but once more to the neighbourhood of France and the land-mass of Europe. One of the reasons for planning a nature reserve along the cliffs of the Isle of Wight is the local abundance of another butterfly on the edge of its range – this time the Glanville Fritillary, which so far as we are concerned now seems confined to the Wight. Another such butterfly, the Lulworth Skipper, has its English headquarters from Swanage to Weymouth, strictly along the coastal fringe. Perhaps it should have been called the Durdle Skipper, since the first specimen was captured actually above the arch of Durdle Door, west of Lulworth, on an August day in 1832. Dorset, too, nourishes a number of plants belonging properly to the Mediterranean, exotics of the coast or cliffs. The one most easily noticed is the Golden Samphire (*Inula crithmoides*), blossoming in summer and autumn along the cliffs between Portland – itself an especial home for rare plants – to Swanage. A Wessex plant with southern affinities, a very much rarer species of the New Forest, is the wild gladiolus (*Gladiolus illyricus*), resembling the garden gladiolus about as much as a Derby winner resembles an elephant. To these one might add for exoticism the rare sand-lizard and the rare smooth-snake (the snake feeds on the lizard, *inter alia*), which live a restricted life on the Hampshire and Dorset heaths.

The cliffs of Dorset and the Isle of Wight have their sea-birds and cliff-birds – puffin, guillemot, razorbill, cormorant, shag, lesser black-backed gull, raven and peregrine on the south-western chalk cliffs of the Wight; peregrine, raven, razorbill and guillemot again on the Dorset cliffs. By contrast the heathy shores around Poole Harbour and on either side of the Solent have nesting colonies of the black-headed gull – gulleries, for example, on Rempstone Heath below Corfe, at Keyhaven behind Hurst Castle, at Needs Oar Point farther east at the mouth of the Beaulieu River, and across the water in the flat, estuarine desolation of the Newtown River, for the Isle of Wight faces low towards the land, high towards the sea. And there are coastal marshes along the Solent, in Poole Harbour and in Christchurch Harbour for waders, ducks and geese.

Inland, on the chalk, life tends naturally to a sameness as the same territorial and scenic conditions are repeated with less dramatic variation. The downs have their characteristic flowers from the stemless thistle to the gentian (*Gentiana amarella*) and various species of orchid, larks disappear into a deep sky, badgers have their earths in escarpment and hanger. There are special birds of the Hampshire and Wiltshire downland – corn-bunting, lapwing, the improbable-looking stone-curlew, the hobby; and in some seasons you can hear the peculiar triple call, 'wet my feet', of the migratory quail. The quail is a running rather than a flying bird, proper to a rolling champaign. Wiltshire's saddest loss has been the bustard, four feet from bill to tail, and a fowl, as Gilbert White described it, so shy that it 'does not care to admit a person within so many furlongs'. Formerly, it ran the length and breadth of Salisbury Plain, though if it existed now it would find itself running into a combine harvester or a line of tanks on exercise. I can at least claim to have known the man who claimed in his turn to have eaten, when he was a child, part of the roast leg of the last bustard shot on the plain – but the bird, I suppose, must have been a straggler from across the Channel.

THE DRY FLY

The geographical peculiarities of Wessex neither add much to nor subtract much from the sports which can be enjoyed in most parts of

At Stourhead in Wiltshire, the National Trust preserves the finest surviving landscape garden of the 18th century, adorned with grotto, lakes and temples.

Great Britain, except for yachting under the shelter of the Isle of Wight and fishing for trout and grayling in the chalk streams of Wiltshire and Hampshire – dry fly, and some of the most delicate, rewarding, and incidentally most expensive by the yard of any fishing to be had. Stockbridge on the Test is as famous for large trout skilfully brought to the net on 4-x gut as Hambledon for cricket; and the fishermen you see there going in and out of the Grosvenor Hotel should be the Comptons, Bradmans and W. G. Graces of the fishing world, since the hotel is the H.Q. of the Houghton Fishing Club, known as Britain's most select and exclusive circle of anglers. I should hesitate to estimate the cost per trout per season for a rod on one of the best beats of the Test or the Itchen. Trout or no, the sight of a chalk stream running between the meadows, slow but not sluggish, and clear to the pebbles between the white patches of water crowfoot, is not to be neglected among the good things of Wessex.

It would be wrong, as I suggested at the beginning, to call Wessex a province linked by a common sentiment. A Wiltshireman feels no particular kinship with someone from Dorset or someone from Hampshire. Least of all does a countryman from the Isle of Wight feel a kinship with any of them; and Hampshire, with its resorts and its factories and docks, its service men and their families, is acquiring a mixed rather than a 'native' population. A floating population, too. The railways have not helped to unite the counties. They run swiftly through Hampshire to join London to its outer suburbs of Southampton and Portsmouth, Bournemouth and the Isle of Wight. They cut through Wiltshire towards the west, only turning aside as an afterthought into Dorset, the most self-contained and clannish of these counties of Wessex. One can go more quickly from Ventnor in the Isle of Wight to London than (about half the distance) from North Wiltshire to the coast. Between Devizes and Salisbury is the width of Salisbury Plain; and the trains go round – in none too much of a hurry. Dickens was the child of a clerk in the navy pay-office at Portsmouth. When he was two his parents moved back to London. Hardy was the son of a Dorset builder, Barnes of a Dorset farmer: they remained content with the county they were rooted in. The contrast is a fair one, and applies even now; and though more and more people gather behind the Isle of Wight and around Bournemouth, and may push more and more inland, one may doubt if there is ever going to be a true marriage here of the transformed coast and the ancient hinterland, or if the Wessex I have written of will ever look to Southampton as a capital. The natural cast of this countryside and the older lines of its development will remain too strong. Most of Dorset and Wiltshire will keep to themselves as two of the most emphatically rural of English counties.

THE TOURS

Salisbury Plain near Wyle, Wiltshire.

If you cannot wander through Wessex at full leisure, the six tours described below should give you the essence of town and country-side with the least expenditure of time.

They have been prepared with the aid of local experts; each of the six routes offers a comfortable day by car or coach, or a journey of two or three days if you are bicycling.

The routes are based on three centres – Dorchester, Southampton and Salisbury. Any of these may equally well be chosen as a starting point for two of the tours; but to make reference easier they are numbered as though Dorchester had been chosen as the first centre. A map showing these will be found on the next page.

The tours are illustrated by special strip maps, somewhat after the style of road maps first made by John Ogilby (1600–1676), who called himself 'His Majesty's Cosmographer and Geographic Printer.' He produced the first comprehensive map of English roads.

The route is read from bottom to top of the page so that it can be followed as you go. The captions at the side indicate things of especial interest.

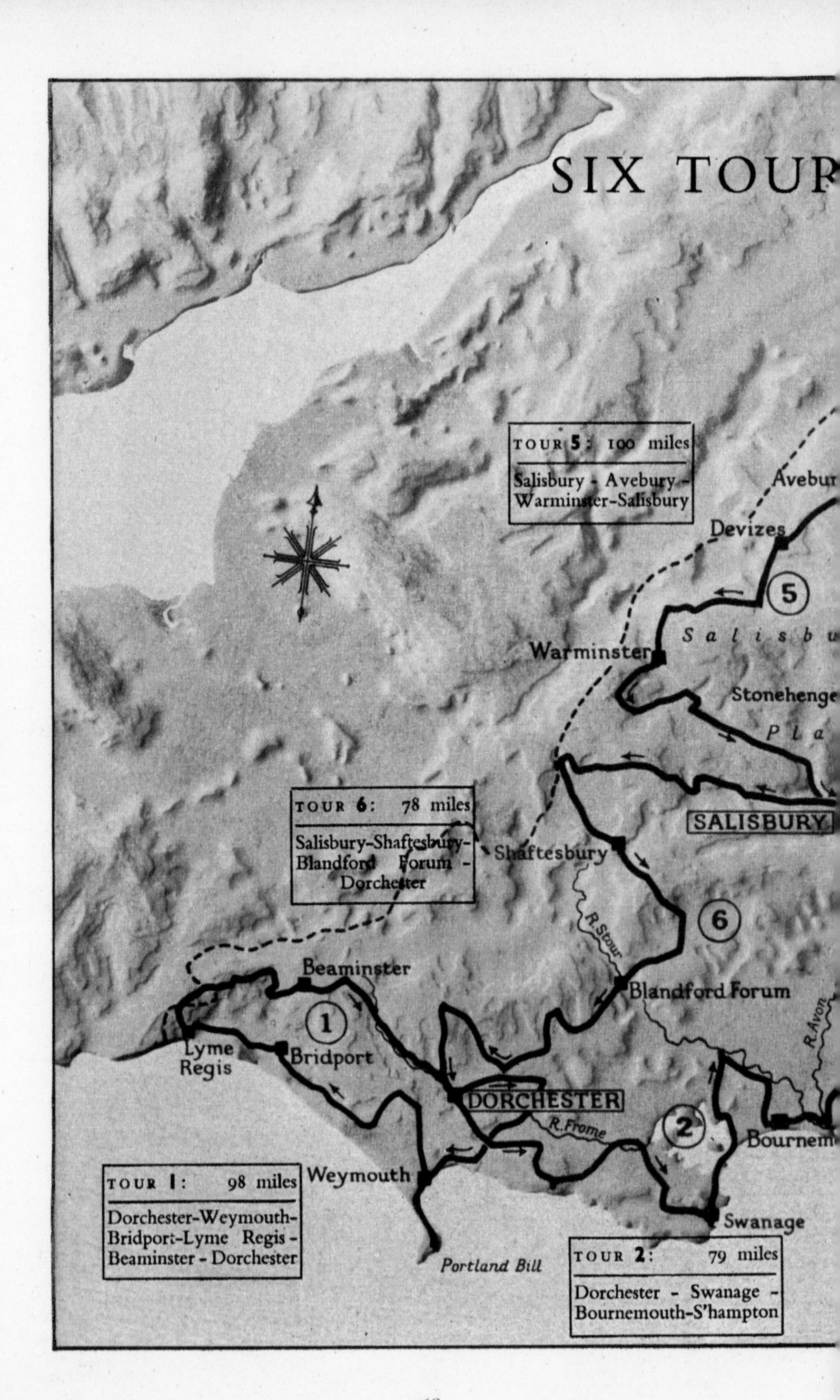
SIX TOUR
TOUR 5: 100 miles
Salisbury - Avebury - Warminster-Salisbury
Devizes
Warminster
Stonehenge
SALISBURY
TOUR 6: 78 miles
Salisbury-Shaftesbury-Blandford Forum - Dorchester
Shaftesbury
R. Stour
Blandford Forum
R. Avon
Beaminster
Lyme Regis
Bridport
DORCHESTER
R. Frome
Weymouth
Portland Bill
Swanage
TOUR 1: 98 miles
Dorchester-Weymouth-Bridport-Lyme Regis - Beaminster - Dorchester
TOUR 2: 79 miles
Dorchester - Swanage - Bournemouth-S'hampton

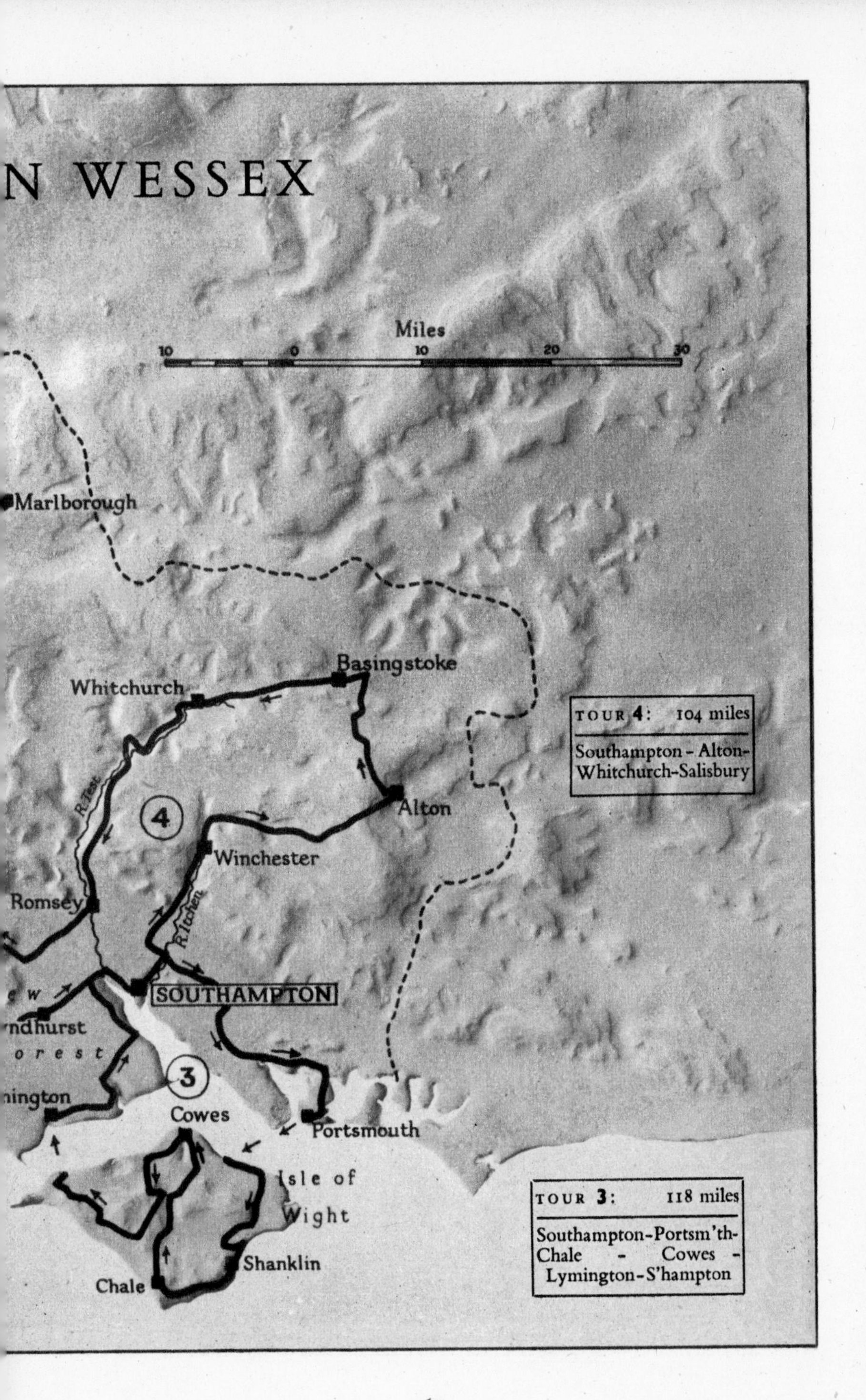
N WESSEX
Miles
10
0
10
20
30
Marlborough
Basingstoke
Whitchurch
R. Test
4
Alton
Winchester
R. Itchen
Romsey
SOUTHAMPTON
ew
ndhurst
orest
3
nington
Cowes
Portsmouth
Isle of
Wight
Shanklin
Chale
TOUR 4: 104 miles
Southampton - Alton-
Whitchurch-Salisbury
TOUR 3: 118 miles
Southampton-Portsm'th-
Chale - Cowes -
Lymington-S'hampton

Tour 1
Dorchester – Bridport – Dorchester
98 miles

For Abbotsbury and abbey remains and exquisitely placed swannery, see gazetteer. Do not miss Lord Ilchester's exotic gardens (open daily).

Below the tower on Winterborne Steepleton church, look for the Saxon flying angel.

Weymouth Town Hall Clock Tower

Osmington: a pretty village of thatch with a pretty stone vicarage in which Archdeacon Fisher entertained Constable, who made sketches here for his National Gallery picture of Weymouth Bay.

Puddletown; a church with superlative chapel of medieval effigies; Jacobean fittings, early canvas buckets of Sun Fire Office.

Dorchester: The route leaves by A.35 form Dorchester, the county town (see gazetteer).

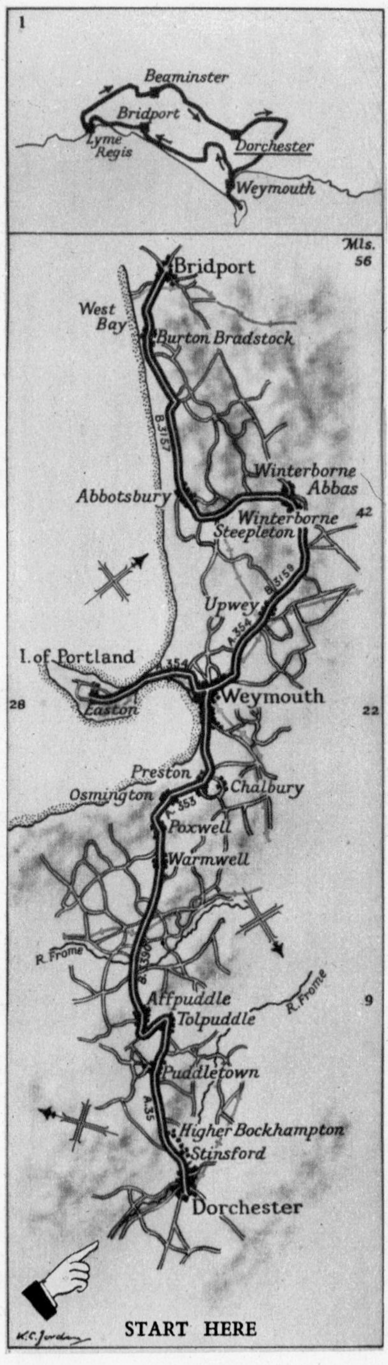

Bridport

Bridport. Nets made here go to every corner of the world.

Coming down to Burton Bradstock, the sharp yellow cliffs and the sea gleam ahead.

Abbotsbury St Catherine's Chapel

The road to the Isle of Portland crosses the Chesil Bank, skirting the naval harbour.

Half a mile right, beyond Preston, a byroad to stone-dyked Chalbury, an Iron Age hill fort. View across to White Horse Hill, along which George III rides on a charger (p. 19).

At Tolpuddle we pass the cottages built by the Trades Union Congress in memory of the Tolpuddle Martyrs (p. 52).

A right hand turn leads to Stinsford church where Thomas Hardy's heart is buried with his two wives among other Hardy gravestones under a yew.

Tour 1
Concluded

Note Frampton church, mixture of classic and Gothic. Family history of Brownes and Sheridans in memorials. Read pompous virtues of John Brown (died 1750), Recorder of Dorchester.

Mapperton ($\frac{1}{2}$ mile right). Isolated and charming group of church, Tudor manor house and stables.

Beaminster. Good 17th- and 18th-century monuments in church and rich figure carving on tower.

Skirting Pilsdon Pen (907 ft.) crowned by Iron Age Fort. Magnificent Marshwood panoramas.

LymeRegis : GunCliff

At Chideock (where cottage netting for the Bridport factories is carried on, e.g. making pockets for billiard tables), turn left for half mile visit to Seatown and views of the great 600 ft. cliffs of Golden Cap.

Dorchester

(See gazetteer).

Our route sweeps back down A.356 with little to attract notice except the large wireless transmitter and drops at Maiden Newton into the Frome Valley.

Toller Down Gate. $\frac{1}{2}$ mile up A.356 the horse chestnut entrance to Urles Farm, where Thomas Hollis is buried (see p. 54).

We turn right at Broadwindsor. Note the yellow and brown of the stone houses.

A steep climb out of Charmouth and a steep descent to Lyme Regis, the last Dorset town.

Charmouth. Pretty villa architecture of early 19th century (see gazetteer).

Descending from Morecombelake, sea views left and glimpses right to the inland grazing meadows of the Marshwood Vale.

Tour 2
Dorchester – Bournemouth – Southampton
79 miles

Forest again. These portions of the New Forest on either side of Lyndhurst do not show it at its most primitive and most intimate.

Christchurch Priory

Bournemouth, rhododendrons, pines, ilexes, large hotels, the faint noise of bridge hands being dealt, the youngest large town in Great Britain (see gazetteer).

After crossing narrow clay-mine railway, the tumbled fragments of Corfe Castle appear, and the delicious stony village of Corfe (see gazetteer and p. 24).

A detour right through the fine park of Came House (18th century) to Winterborne Came church.

We leave by A.352, crossing the Frome by an 18th-century bridge.

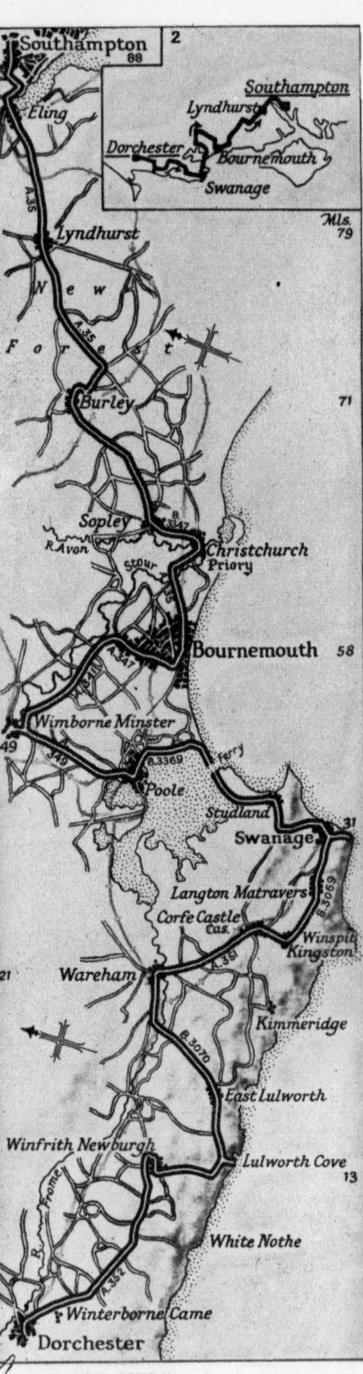

Southampton (see gazetteer).

Eling Church (¼ mile right on the edge of Southampton Water). Memorial by Rysbrack.

Cottages at Lyndhurst

We turn right, below Sopley Park, crossing low meadows on to the heaths of the New Forest (see gazetteer).

For Wimborne Minster, see gazetteer.

Poole: Custom House

The grey town of Swanage, with exhilarating view north across the blue bay to the chalk cliffs.

The splendid cliff scenery between White Nothe and Lulworth can be surveyed only on foot or by bicycle, taking the turning below Owermoigne and then along from Holworth House to Lulworth (see gazetteer).

Tour **3**

Southampton – Chale – Southampton

118 miles

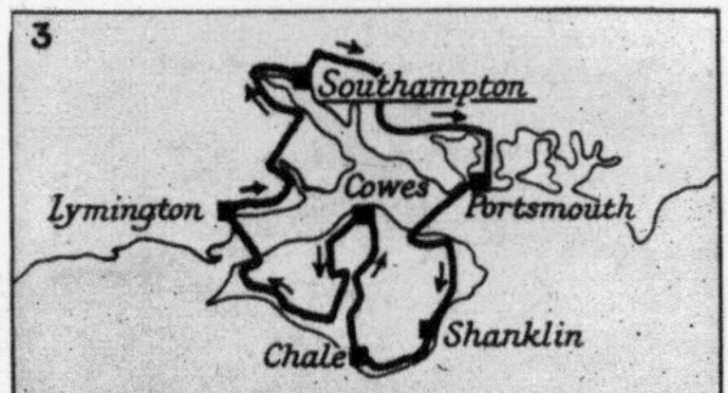

St Catherine's Old Lighthouse

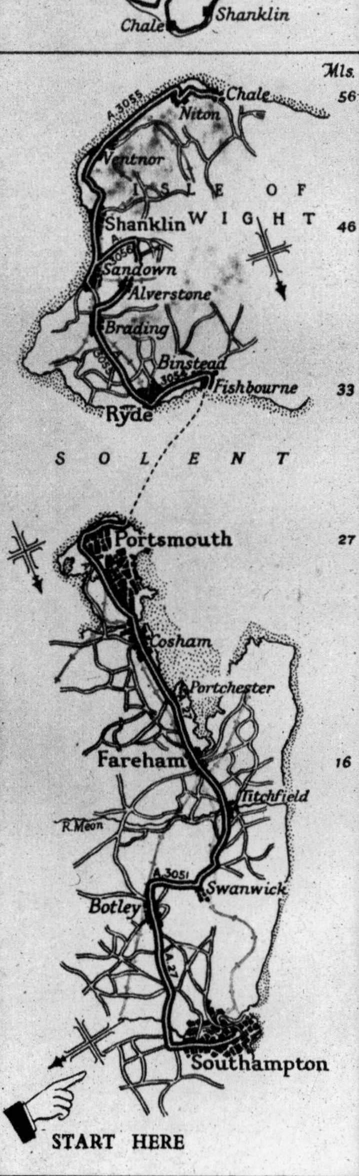

A lovely descent into the neat cleanliness of Ventnor.

Sandown and Shanklin are two more holiday centres.

Note in Binstead churchyard the carved tombstone of Thomas Swell, a smuggler shot in 1785.

The passenger-ferry to the Isle of Wight sails from Portsmouth to Ryde. But the car-ferry leaves from Southsea, Portsmouth's holiday centre, and sails to Fishbourne.

Portchester Castle

From the stones of Titchfield Abbey, 'Place House,' now a ruin, was built in the 16th century.

Most of the flat arable land between Botley and Fareham is devoted to market-gardening. Fields with their neat rows of produce on all sides.

High up on St Catherine's Hill stands a 14th-century lighthouse which was once tended by a priest.

Ryde betrays the Island's chief 'industry' – catering for holiday-makers.

Portsmouth: Dickens' birthplace

Although much of the town is ugly and uninteresting, Portsmouth, the birthplace of Charles Dickens, and steeped in naval history, has much to detain the visitor.

Strawberries are one of the chief crops in this district.

A ferry service operates between Southampton and the Isle of Wight (Cowes), but in order to see some of Southern Hampshire first we sail from Portsmouth (see gazetteer).

Tour 3
Concluded

Many wooden ships for the Royal Navy were built below at the small village of Bucklers Hard.

Beaulieu Abbey Cloisters

Yarmouth, with its delightful harbour, was the most important island port in the Middle Ages.

Mottistone is one of the loveliest villages in the Isle of Wight.

Parkhurst Forest, an ancient royal forest, chiefly oak and fir, lies to the right of the road from Cowes. Parkhurst Prison stands at its south-east corner.

Osborne House, near Whippingham, was one of Queen Victoria's favourite residences. Here she died in 1901.

The scenery north of Chale is typical of the southern part of the Island. Rolling downs radiate from the central chalk ridge and contrast sharply with the flat, wooded country in the north.

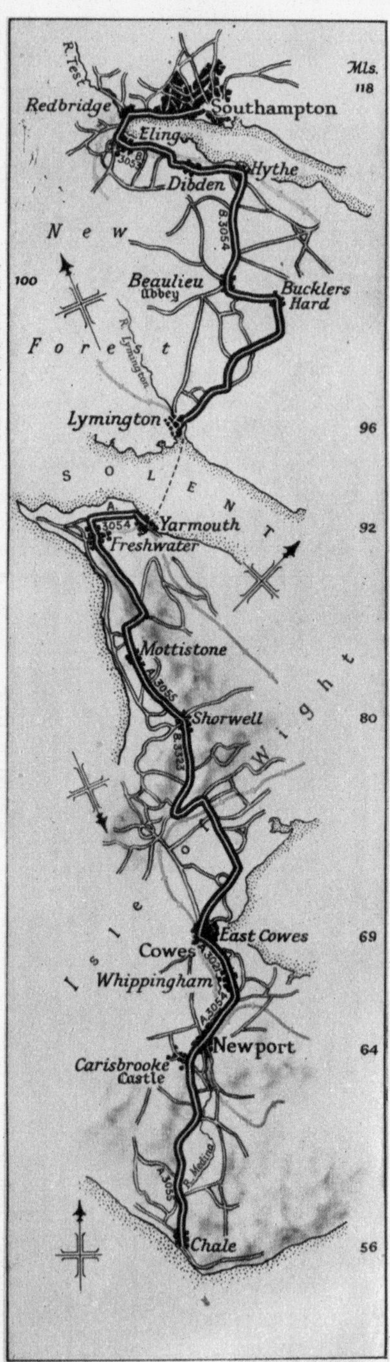

Southampton: West Gate

Southampton (see gazetteer).

Note the Tudor castle, companion to Hurst Castle across the Solent, which you see as the ferry takes you from the Isle of Wight over to Lymington.

From the downs near Freshwater, we get a good view of the Needles.

From the top of Brighstone Down fine views of sea and down.

Within sight of Carisbrooke Castle again, we turn down to Shorwell.

Cowes is the centre of British yachting and the home of the Royal Yacht Squadron.

Carisbrooke Castle Gate

For the noble ruin of Carisbrooke Castle, in which Charles I was imprisoned before his execution in 1649, see page 51.

Tour **4**

Southampton – Whitchurch – Salisbury

104 miles

Overton is a village of watercress-growing.

From Whitchurch into Romsey there are water-meadows on all sides, in contrast to the open downs.

Basingstoke is a busy railway and agricultural centre.

Near Basing are the ruins and earthworks of Basing House, the ancient seat of the Paulet family.

Place names show that much of this land once belonged to the Church – Abbot's Worthy, Itchen Abbas, Bishop's Sutton.

Winchester: St Catherine's Hill

This main road through Otterbourne and Compton follows the old Roman road into Winchester.

George Kemp, one of Marconi's assistants in early wireless experiments, lies in South Stoneham churchyard.

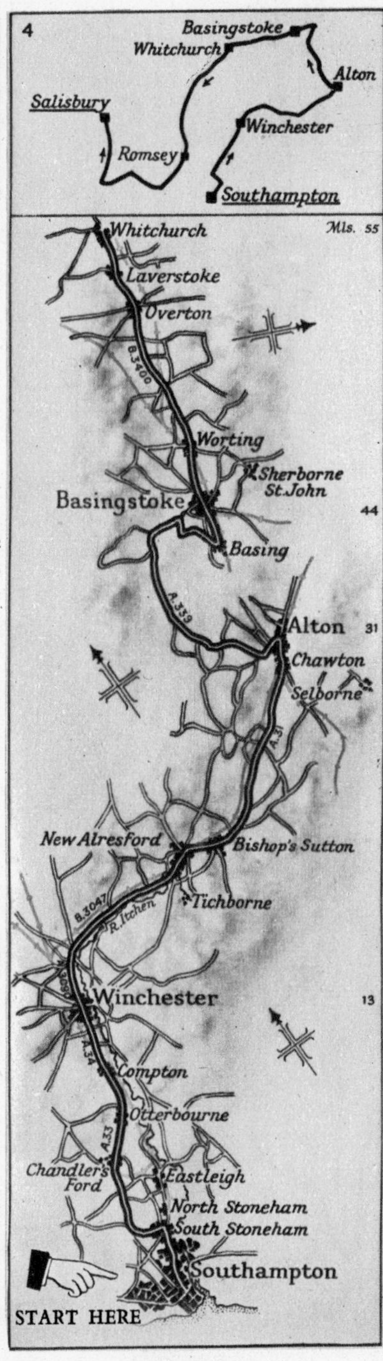

The church at Whitchurch has a fine Tudor memorial.

Paper for Bank of England notes has been made at Laverstoke since 1724, in mills belonging to the Portal family.

Two miles north of Basingstoke at Sherborne St John is one of Hampshire's most beautiful country houses, The Vyne.

Selborne Church

Some 5 miles south-east of Alton is Selborne, where Gilbert White (1720-1793), the author of *The Natural History of Selborne*, was vicar.

Winchester, the ancient capital of England (see gazetteer).

At Otterbourne the road begins to climb on to the chalk downs, which form the geological backbone of the county.

Southampton: Bar Gate

Tour 4
Concluded

Salisbury, perhaps the most beautiful county town in England (see gazetteer).

Breamore has one of the finest Saxon churches in the south of England.

Breamore Church

A mile south of Brook is the Rufus Stone, marking the spot where William Rufus, King of England, was killed by an arrow in A.D. 1100.

Soon after leaving Romsey for Cadnam we begin to enter the New Forest, which covers the south-west corner of Hampshire.

Stockbridge is the H.Q. of the celebrated 'Houghton Club' for fly-fishermen (see p. 65).

Wherwell, celebrated for its thatch, is called by its inhabitants 'Horrell.'

Our road follows the Test through Wherwell, Stockbridge and Romsey, whence it flows to Southampton Water.

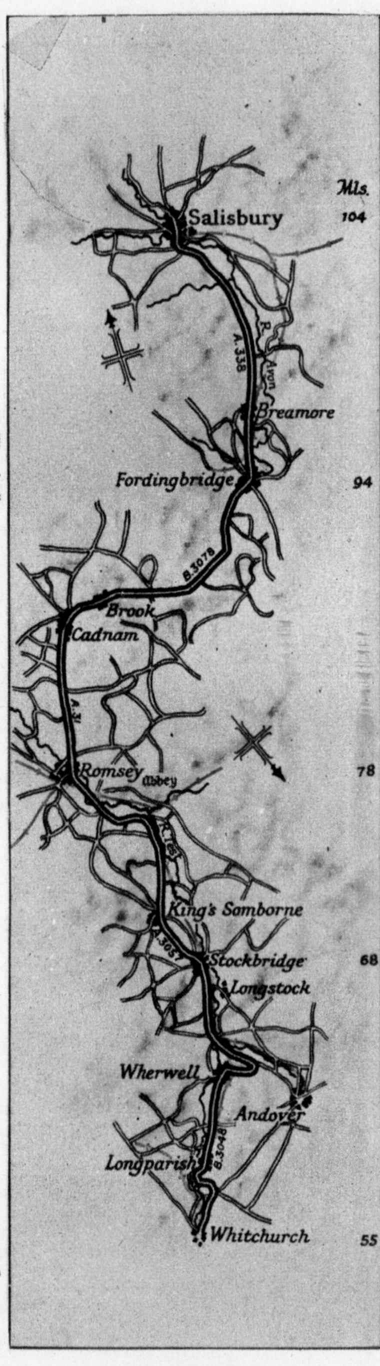

Salisbury: Harnham Gate

Soon after leaving Breamore we pass out of Hampshire into Wiltshire.

Fordingbridge is an ancient Forest town whose name betrays the reason for the original settlement.

The Rufus Stone

For the Romanesque Abbey church of Romsey, see gazetteer. Romsey is a town of fine old inns.

Below King's Somborne the road and railway both follow the easiest natural route by clinging to the river valley.

Andover, 4 miles west of Longparish, is an ancient borough at an important road junction.

Longparish lives up to its name: its attractive cottages straggle for more than a mile along the main road.

Tour **5**
Salisbury – Avebury – Salisbury
100 miles

Marlborough, its long street full of good 18th- and early 19th-century buildings, antique shops, book shops and tea shops (see gazetteer).

Marlborough College

Note from time to time the daub walls, whitewashed and protectively thatched, typical of stoneless areas of Wessex.

On our detour left along A.303, Stonehenge comes wonderfully into view between two forking roads (see pp. 14-16).

Amesbury Church

Modern Salisbury almost reaches out along A.345 to the fortified hill of Old Sarum (i.e. Old Salisbury).

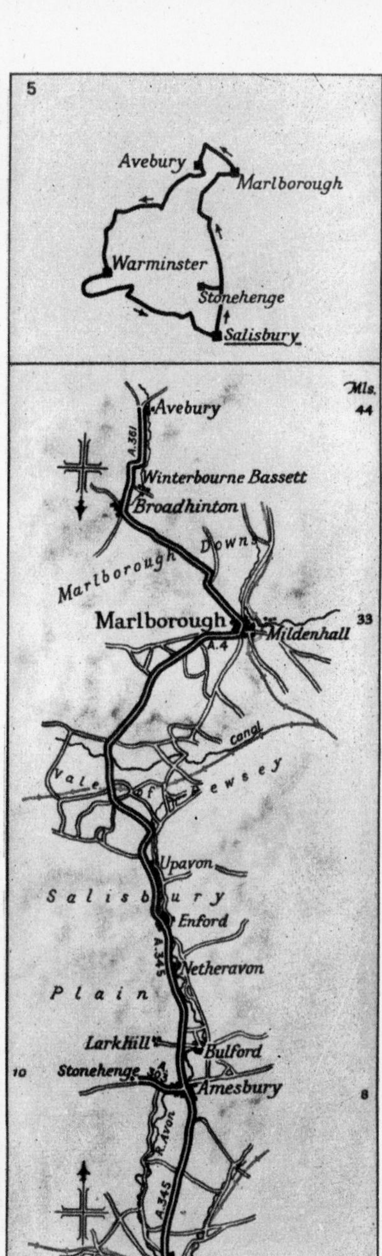

The low, barrow-pimpled outline of Windmill Hill with its causewayed camp soon appears on the right, after which the road enters Avebury (see gazetteer).

A.361 now runs along parallel with the downs, from which much sarsen has been dragged down through the centuries for building.

Chalk downs ahead again. Note the bold white horse in the hillside designed in 1812 by a travelling painter who was afterwards hanged.

We now leave the downs for the fertile Vale of Pewsey on the greensand.

Back through Amesbury. As A.345 rises past modern houses, stop on the left for Woodhenge (see p. 15).

The route quickly climbs to the rolling upland of Salisbury Plain, descending to the Avon at the old, but now shabby, military-seeming town of Amesbury.

Old Sarum: Castle foundations

Tour **5**
Concluded

A.36 joins A.30 for the 3 miles or so into Salisbury at Wilton (see gazetteer).

Two miles left up A.303 is the huge Iron Age, elder-grown earthwork of Yarnbury Castle.

Note the fine yew in the churchyard of Longbridge Deverill.

Warminster: Church of St Denys

The road (B.3089) now runs along under steep chalk hills, the northern escarpment of Salisbury Plain, through pretty villages of which the most notable is Edington (see p. 46).

For Devizes, clean, cheerful town, good 18th-century buildings, inns, museum, etc. (see gazetteer).

Leaving Avebury we have a glimpse left of dark green Silbury Hill, the huge, unexplained, tumulus-like, prehistoric mound.

Wilton Church

'Boyton church, has effigy of 13th-century crusader in memorial chapel built by his brother.

Warminster, a pretty, busy country town, with good inns. The Marquis of Bath's celebrated 16th-century mansion of Longleat lies outside the town (along A.362) see gazetteer.

Beyond Bratton the prehistoric camp of Bratton Castle is prominent above the road; and below it the Westbury White Horse (1778).

Off the chalk again we cross the lower part of the Vale of Pewsey. Note the rich medieval house in Potterne, which was restored by the Victorian artist, George Richmond.

Silbury Hill

Tour **6**

Salisbury –
Blandford Forum –
Dorchester

78 miles

Cerne Abbas : Abbey Gateway

We go off right at the Blue Vinney Inn (named after the Dorset cheese).
Farnham. The Pitt-Rivers museum, bygones, pottery archaeology, primitive art, Benin bronzes (see p. 58 and gazetteer).
Shaftesbury (Shaston on milestones) lies ahead on its high ridge (see gazetteer).
We enter Dorset after Zeals, crossing a vale under the chalk hills.
Here we turn left into the old domain of Beckford's Fonthill Abbey (p. 48)
Note at Teffont Evias the stream running along the road by the cottages, a typical Wessex feature.
We enter Wilton (gazetteer and p. 48) along the wall of the grounds of Wilton House, the seat of the Earls of Pembroke.
We leave the city by A.30 along the Nadder Valley.

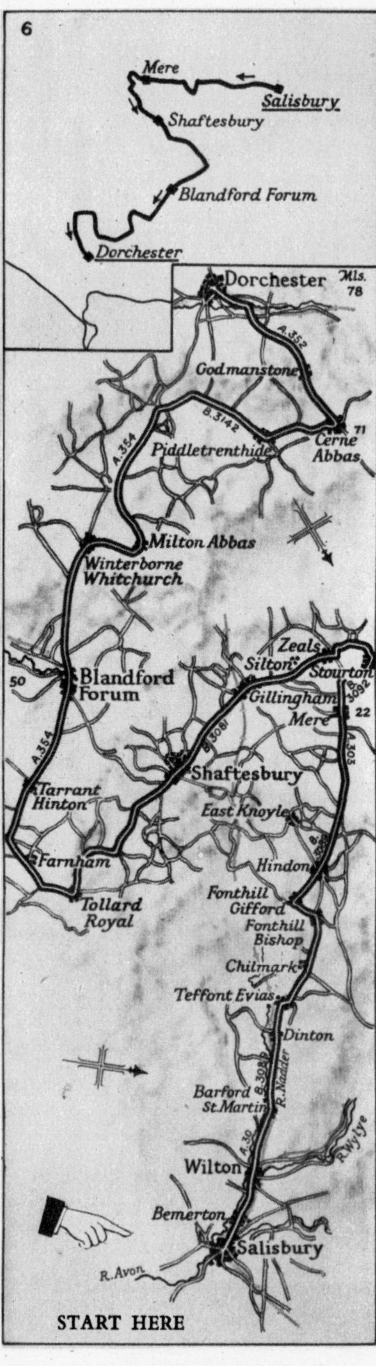

We end at Dorchester, coming in by the seated statue of Thomas Hardy.
At Godmanstone, the Smith's Arms Inn, where church, mill, road and river come together. A thatched doll's house inn, converted from a forge.
Down to Cerne Abbas. For the abbey ruins, details of this pretty village and the unbashful Cerne Giant see p. 46.

Blandford

Stourton. Here are Stourhead House and the landscape gardens (now National Trust).
Hindon, a pleasant inn (The Lamb) and a Victorian church of Chilmark stone.
Chilmark. A village of the grey Chilmark stone with a finely spired church.
An unusual tomb in the church of Barford St Martin, a painting of a woman in her winding sheet.

Bemerton Church & Vicarage

A GAZETTEER TO WESSEX

BY GEOFFREY GRIGSON

NOTE

This is a selective gazetteer of places and points of special interest or character – a topographical anthology. The numbers show the pages on which main references to these occur; bold type refers to illustrations.

For information about hotels, early closing days, markets, garages, etc., readers should refer to publications of the British Travel and Holidays Association, the British Hotels and Restaurants Association, the Royal Automobile Club, the Automobile Association or the Cyclists' Touring Club.

Many towns issue comprehensive lists of accommodation and guide booklets which can be obtained from the local Information Office. Further useful advice is also available in the area Holiday Guides published by British Railways.

ABBOTSBURY, *Dorset*. **21.**
This village near the coast is of the first interest. Of the Benedictine abbey, little remains. But see St Catherine's Chapel overlooking the Fleet and the sea and the monk's barn (also 15th century). Lord Ilchester's sub-tropical gardens are open daily. So is the swannery on the edge of the Fleet, best seen in the breeding season, when the dark, trim cygnets are fed in wire pens.
9 m. S.W. of Dorchester.

AFFPUDDLE, *Dorset*
On the one-inch map you will find 'Cullpepper's Dish' marked on Affpuddle Heath. It is the biggest of the many curious swallow-holes on the Dorset heaths, which are among the county's geological oddities. The heaths hereabout have a sombre attraction made more bizarre by gravel digging. Affpuddle church by the Piddle river has unusual oak fittings of 1547.
8 m. E. of Dorchester.

ST ALDHEM'S HEAD, *Dorset*
See Kimmeridge and Swanage.

ALRESFORD, *Hampshire*
New Alresford is a small town with 18th-century houses. Mary Russell Mitford (1787-1855), who wrote *Our Village*, was born in one of these houses in the tree-shaded Broad Street, which leads to the lake made by a medieval bishop for the navigation of the Itchen. Beyond the lake the village of Old Alresford, where there are good monuments in the 18th-century church.
7½ m. E. of Winchester.

ALTON, *Hampshire*
A brewing town among the hop-fields, with the Curtis Museum (rural 'bygones', etc.) and a notable parish church, 15th-century and Norman, containing wall paintings, carvings, and furnishings of various ages. See the brass to Colonel Boles, killed in the church in the Civil War. 18 m. E. of Winchester.

AVEBURY, *Wiltshire*. **3**, 10–14.
Stone circles, Silbury Hill, Windmill Hill, and a well-known Museum. Avebury is one of the essential places to visit in Wessex; and the visit should certainly include the brief walk to the top of Windmill Hill, if not for the archaeological remnants then for the superb panorama of the ancient countryside of the Beaker folk. There is excellent walking on the downs both on the Marlborough and the Devizes side of the village.
8¼ m. N.E. of Devizes.

AVINGTON, *Hampshire*
The small church (1779) alongside Avington Park should be visited for its mahogany fittings and memorials. The mansion belongs to the Shelleys; and there is a memorial to Shelley's brother in the church. 4 m. N.E. of Winchester.

BADBURY RINGS, *Dorset*. **8**.
Among the most scenically moving of the Iron Age camps of Wessex, alongside B3082 between Blandford and Wimborne. Three ramparts and a central plantation of pines.
5½ m. S.E. of Blandford.

BASING, *Hampshire*
The two things to see in this village are the church and the earthworks and ruins of Basing House, once the seat of the Paulets, Marquises of Winchester. With Cromwell in command, Basing House was captured in 1645 after a long siege; and destroyed. The church contains a fine series of monuments to the Paulets and their descendants. Note Flaxman's bust of the 6th Duke of Bolton. 2 m. E. of Basingstoke.

BEAULIEU, *Hampshire*
The remains of the Cistercian abbey are charmingly placed by the Beaulieu River. They include the Lavatory, the Refectory (now the parish church) and the Dormitory. Also the Gatehouse, now the home of Lord Montagu of Beaulieu. At St Leonard's near-by see the ruins of the vast abbey barn and the grange chapel.

At Buckler's Hard, ships-of-the-line were built from New Forest oak in the 18th century, the shipwrights living in the two rows of pretty brick cottages.
13 m. S. of Southampton.

BEMERTON, *Wiltshire*
The saintly poet George Herbert (1593-1633) is buried in the little flint church outside Salisbury. Note the lines by Herbert on the parsonage wall opposite. The larger church of St John (1860) was built as a memorial to Herbert.
1½ m. W. of Salisbury.

BERE REGIS, *Dorset*
A good Dorset church of the 15th century with a splendidly complex hammer-beam roof from which large angels look down on the congregation. 10½ m. E. of Dorchester.

BISHOPS CANNINGS, *Wiltshire*. 41.
A large and admirable spired church under the downs, 13th, 14th and 15th centuries, which belonged to the bishops of Salisbury. Wansdyke runs across the downs nearby.
3 m. N.E. of Devizes.

BISHOPSTONE, *Wiltshire*
A 14th-century church – a fine building in itself with the added interests of a cloister, a tomb by Pugin to the rector who restored the church and was killed in 1842 by the fall of stone work during the building of Benjamin Ferrey's church of East Grafton. The rector installed the painted pulpit. 6 m. S.W. of Salisbury.

BLANDFORD FORUM, *Dorset*. 54.
One of the most delightful small towns of Wessex (or Great Britain) classically resurrected after the fire of 1731 by the master-builders John and William Bastard (of whom there are portraits in the Town Hall). See especially the Town Hall, the church, the *Greyhound Inn* (now a bank), the *Red Lion*, the Pump-House ('In Remembrance of God's dreadful visitation by fire'). Note tablet in the church to George Vince, Antarctic explorer with Captain Scott.
17 m. N.E. of Dorchester.

BLUE POOL, *Dorset*
An old clay pit (for the clay pits and mines see p. 60) west of A351 between Wareham and Corfe. Unbelievably sapphire among pines. Discreetly turned into a pleasure garden with teas and exotic birds in aviaries.
2¾ m. S. of Wareham.

BOARHUNT, *Hampshire*
Here is one of the Saxon churches of Wessex, of flint and rubble. 7½ m. N.W. of Portsmouth.

HIGHER BOCKHAMPTON, *Dorset*. 50.
Hardy's birthplace.
3 m. N.E. of Dorchester.

BOKERLY DYKE, *Dorset*
Rampart and ditch of the late Roman period. See Tollard Royal.

BOURNEMOUTH, *Hampshire*. **38**, 56.
Villas, mansions, hotels, boarding houses, pines and rhododendrons, and long stretches of sand. Bournemouth has a savour of opulence, Victorian, Edwardian and modern, concentrated especially in its churches such as St Peter's (by the Victorian architect G. E. Street) and the Russell Cotes Art Gallery in a mansion overlooking the sands, the vaster hotels and the private houses among trees and flowering shrubs. The art gallery is a remarkable shrine of obsolete taste – pictures, marble statuary and *objets d'art* – with few parallels in Great Britain. The view from the cliff top near the gallery of the long sands, the bathers, the pleasure boats cutting white arcs in the blue sea, make one forget much of the less pleasant urban landscape

of the town. Another of the amenities of Bournemouth is one of the best secondhand bookshops of Wessex. 103 m. S.W. of London.

BOWOOD, *Wiltshire*
Superb landscape park, formal garden and mansion of the Marquis of Lansdowne, under the downs. The gardens are frequently open in the summer. Note the artificial lake, the temple among the trees and the cascade after a landscape by Gaspard Poussin. The bacon factory town of Calne nearby is of little interest.
14 m. W. of Marlborough.

BRAMLEY, *Hampshire*
A good church with early wall paintings, brasses, furniture and the Brocas chapel (1801) with a monument to Bernard Brocas by the neo-classic sculptor Thomas Banks.
5 m. N. of Basingstoke.

BRAMSHILL PARK, *Hampshire*
Bramshill House is a very fine Jacobean mansion built by Lord Zouch (1607-1612) of rosy coloured brick. 10 m. N.E. of Basingstoke.

BREAMORE, *Hampshire*
Here is the stumpy Saxon church of St Mary, with a rood and a Saxon inscription. Some way off the road on Breamore Down (difficult to find without a one-inch map) is the circular turf labyrinth known as the Breamore Mizmaze. Half-a-mile north-west of the maze is a portion of Grim's Ditch (q.v.). 8 m. S. of Salisbury.

BRIDPORT, *Dorset*. **13, 17**.
A town with an air of sleepy antiquity which conceals its busy share in world trade. Italian hemp and Egyptian cotton are turned into nets and fishing requisites for the fisheries of most countries of the world. Note the Georgian façade of Gundry's factory which conceals a large range of modern net sheds and machines.
The little windy harbour of West Bay is 1½ miles south of Bridport, between crumpled fossiliferous yellow cliffs of great beauty.
9½ m. E. of Lyme Regis.

BROMHAM, *Wiltshire*
The 15th-century church in this village contains the exquisite Bayntun Chapel. Tom Moore the poet is buried in the churchyard under a modern Celtic cross. 4 m. N.W. of Devizes.

BUCKLERS HARD, *Hampshire*
See Beaulieu.

BURGHCLERE, *Hampshire*
For the Oratory of All Souls, with paintings of the Salonika front by Stanley Spencer, see p. 51. The Oratory is not at Burghclere village, but some distance off by Highclere Station. Climb the noble chalk eminence of Beacon Hill (859 feet), alongside A34 to Winchester. It is crowned by an Iron Age camp. 6 m. S. of Newbury.

CERNE ABBAS, *Dorset*. 46.
Monastic village between buttocks of chalk. Good houses. The Gatehouse (15th-century) of the Abbey can be seen in a private garden. The odd *pièce de résistance* is the Cerne Giant (National Trust). 7¾ m. N.W. of Dorchester.

CHALBURY CAMP, *Dorset*
Iron Age camp with stone ramparts above Weymouth Bay. 3 m. N.E. of Weymouth.

CHARLTON MARSHALL, *Dorset*
Early 18th century church, small but of great charm with excellent woodwork. Possibly designed by Thomas Bastard, father of the Bastards who rebuilt so much of Blandford (q.v.). 2 m. S.E. of Blandford.

CHARMOUTH, *Dorset*. **12**.
On Charmouth see Jane Austen in *Persuasion*. The flavour of Miss Austen has not disappeared. Pretty villas of the Regency period climb the hill; and the 1836 church has a charming interior. Fossiliferous cliffs of interest and beauty.
2¾ m. E. of Lyme Regis.

CHAWTON, *Hampshire*. 52.
A place of pilgrimage for lovers of Jane Austen, who wrote *Emma* and *Persuasion* in the red brick cottage in the village. See also Steventon.
1½ m. S. of Alton.

CHESIL BEACH or BANK, *Dorset*. **18**.
One of the most dramatic geological curiosities of Dorset. An 18-mile storm beach of pebbles from Chesilton to the Isle of Portland. It is best seen from the Portland heights. Behind it is the 'drowned' area of the Fleet, land which sank in Neolithic times, edged by gentle green slopes never attacked by the sea. Terns rise and fall like snowflakes over the dark waters of the Fleet. Fleet and East Fleet are the scene of much of Meade Falkner's novel *Moonfleet*.

CHIDEOCK, *Dorset*
See Golden Cap.

CHRISTCHURCH, *Hampshire*. **83**.
Christchurch itself has the untidy air of a suburb of Bournemouth, but the long grey Minster is set apart from the streets. It is a church of Norman and Gothic splendours, above the Avon and the yachts. Note especially the Norman nave, the rich Salisbury chantry (early 16th century), the Lady Chapel, and the restored rood screen; and among much else of interest, the marble monument to Shelley by Henry Weeks (1807-1877), the Flaxman memorial to Lady Fitzharris (Maternal Love – a mother reading to her children), the misericord carvings, and the Adoration of the Three Kings in the rood screen. 5½ m. E. of Bournemouth.

CORFE CASTLE, *Dorset*. **22**. **24**, 51.
Noble ruins boldly set on a hill in a gap (*corf*) between taller hills. Castle and village are irresistably surprising (in spite of tea gardens and crowds). 4 m. S. E. of Wareham.

Christchurch Priory, Hampshire, much of it built by the Normans.

CORHAMPTON, *Hampshire*
A Saxon church (11th century) with a stone altar and wall paintings, in the valley of the Meon, one of the minor dry fly streams of Hampshire.
11 m. S. E. of Winchester.

CORSCOMBE and HALSTOCK, *Dorset*. 54.
Farms and fields peculiarly named by the democratical Thomas Hollis.
6 m. N.E. of Beaminster.

CRANBORNE, *Dorset*
The small town which gives its name to the former Royal Forest of Cranborne Chase. Distinguished by a shapely Dorset church and by Cranborne Manor House, once royal property and possibly a hunting lodge built in King John's reign. The medieval house was refashioned in the 17th century, after it came into possession of the Cecil family, who are still the owners. 6½ m. W. of Fordingbridge.

CRANBORNE CHASE, *Wiltshire and Dorset*
See Tollard Royal, Cranborne.

DAMERHAM, *Hampshire*
A Norman church with a tympanum of St George at the Battle of Antioch, and other good details. 3½ m. N.W. of Fordingbridge.

WEST DEAN, *Wiltshire*. 47, **53**.
The old flint church of West Dean, now abandoned, is astoundingly and splendidly stuffed with monuments to the Pierrepoints and Evelyns (17th-century). 8 m. S.E. of Salisbury.

DEVIZES, *Wiltshire*
A pretty, prosperous, active little town, with good inns, churches, and buildings and a tobacco factory. See Norman work in St John's Church (and airy Perpendicular chapel of cool beauty) and the Norman church of St Mary, the town hall by Baldwin of Bath (1808), the mid-19th-century Corn Exchange, the *Bear Inn*, where Sir Thomas Lawrence's father was landlord (relics of Lawrence in the bar), and the small archaeological museum, rich in Wiltshire objects.
14¼ m. S.W. of Marlborough.

DORCHESTER, *Dorset*. 20.
The county town; by origin a Roman town succeeding the Belgic town of Maiden Castle just outside. Though not of great architectural distinction it is a place which has escaped vulgarization and keeps a placid decency. The tree-roofed 'Walks' on the line of the Roman walls are pleasant. The Museum is of much interest. The Roman amphitheatre of Maumbury Rings on the edge of the town was probably by origin a Bronze Age sacred site (*cf.* Avebury, Knowlton Rings). Note the statues of Thomas Hardy seated and William Barnes.
27 m. W. of Bournemouth.

EASTBURY HOUSE, *Dorset*. **49**.
Impressive remnants of mansion by Vanbrugh at Tarrant Gunville.
6 m. N.E of Blandford.

EDINGTON, *Wiltshire*
A long and massive abbey church under the scarp of Salisbury Plain, 14th- and 15th-centuries. A few monuments including one by Chantrey, others of 1400 and 1630. Also a curious neo-Gothic wall tablet in white and black marble with little kneeling figures.
4 m. N.E. of Westbury.

FARLEY *Wiltshire*. 47.
17th-century church with Fox monuments and almshouses.
6 m. E. of Salisbury

FARNBOROUGH, *Hampshire*
A military centre. At Farnborough lived the French Empress Eugénie, who built the tall Roman Catholic church of St Michael over the mausoleum for Napoleon III and the Prince Imperial. 2¼ m. N. of Aldershot.

FARNHAM, *Dorset*
For the Pitt-Rivers museum, see Tollard Royal.

THE FLEET, *Dorset*. 58
See Chesil Beach.

FONTHILL BISHOP, *Wiltshire*. 48.
Celebrated as the place where the millionaire William Beckford built his neo-Gothic abbey, the tower of which crashed. Little of the abbey remains. The road, however, from Fonthill Gifford runs under a great arch along the lake made by Beckford's father. Woods and lake are exquisite. Careful search (enquire locally) will discover the Hermitage and Hermit's Cave made by Beckford on one side of the lake, and his grotto and the caves of the Alpine Garden on the east side. 15 m. W. of Salisbury.

FORDE ABBEY, *Dorset*
On the Axe, where Dorset ends against Devon. Privately owned. The cloister, chapter house great hall and other portions of the medieval abbey remain. State rooms, etc., by Inigo Jones. Tapestries after Raphael in the saloon.
12 m. N. of Lyme Regis.

GOLDEN CAP, *Dorset*
Between Chideock and Charmouth, 618 feet over Wear Cliffs, making one of the most affecting pieces of Dorset coastal scenery, especially in an evening light. Golden sandstone over black Lias clays. Chideock is an attractive little golden village, with its own miniature bathing place at Seatown. 4½ m. W. of Bridport.

GRIM'S DITCH, *Wiltshire*
A double bank and a single ditch in Wiltshire (mainly), Dorset and Hampshire. Probably of earlier date than Bokerly Dyke (*vide* Tollard Royal) and Wansdyke (q.v.), it may have bounded and enclosed grazing areas in the Iron Age or even Late Bronze Age. A fascinating sector to explore is by the yew wood of Great Yews, going about 5 miles south-west of Salisbury on A 354, and then striking across the Downs about one mile S.E. from the fork on Coombe Bissett Down.

HAMBLEDON, *Hampshire*
A cricketer's shrine: the home of the 18th-century Hambledon Club, which legislated for cricket, played here in great style on the ground by the Bat and Ball Inn.
10½ m. N. of Portsmouth.

HAMBLEDON HILL and HOD HILL, *Dorset*. 23.
Crowned with Iron Age camps. Notable scenery. 3¾ m. N.W. of Blandford.

IBBERTON, *Dorset*
Dramatically sited church, reached by a long flight of steps and overlooking the farming Vale of Blackmore. Some of the best of Dorset's inland scenery south along the escarpment to Bulbarrow (902 feet).
6½ m. S. of Sturminster Newton.

IDSWORTH, *Hampshire*
St Hubert's chapel in the parish of Chalton is partly Norman, with 14th-century wall paintings of Herod and St John the Baptist and the legend of St Hubert. Fittings of 17th and 18th centuries. 12 m. N.E. of Portsmouth.

KIMMERIDGE, *Dorset*. 59.
The point is not Kimmeridge village, but the sombre fantasy of Kimmeridge Bay (unspoilt by any development) – black cliffs of shale and clay and bands of rock, flat slabs sliding into the sea; Gad Cliff to the W., a prospect tower to the E. Kimmeridge 'Coal' was mined eastward along Kimmeridge Ledges by Clavell's Hard. A cliff path runs the whole way from the Bay to Hounstout Cliff, St Aldhem's Head (Norman chapel), and then along the top of the vertical cliffs past Winspit and its quarries, Dancing Ledge to Durlston Head, Tilly Whim Caves and Swanage. One of the most extraordinary walks in England, though the walk along the contrasting chalk cliffs, further west to White Nothe has peculiarity of another, though a rather more conventional, beauty. Part of the coast of Purbeck between Worbarrow Bay and Kimmeridge Bay including the mighty Gad Cliff is still shut off as a military training area.
5 m. S.W. of Corfe Castle.

KNOWLTON RINGS, *Dorset*
Nothing in Dorset gives you a stronger sense of the past. Here are earth circles with the ditch *inside*; and in one of them a ruined church. The circles cannot be defensive and are probably Bronze Age sacred enclosures akin to Stonehenge Avebury, etc. 6¾ m. N.E. of Wimborne

LAVERSTOKE, *Hampshire*.
A Test valley parish celebrated for the paper mills which have long made the crisp paper of Bank of England notes. 9 m. E.N.E. of Andover.

St Mary's Church, E. Lulworth, in the grounds of Lulworth Castle.

LONGLEAT, *Wiltshire*
The mansion of the Marquis of Bath, in splendidly wooded grounds, laid out by Capability Brown, and much coloured now by rhododendrons, is regularly open to the public. The building is 16th-century, considerably altered in later periods. Palace is a more fitting word than mansion. Interesting furniture and pictures.
4½ m. W. of Warminster.

LULWORTH COVE, *Dorset.* **25. 85, 90.**
Publicized, painted, approached by a broad smooth road, Lulworth Cove, shaped like a moon a little past the full, is still exaggeratedly curious and exquisite. Here the land extended once further seaward and the Lulworth stream cut through the wall of Portland and Purbeck stone. The sea has entered the gap, widened it a trifle, and carved out the soft beds behind to the chalk. See the Fossil Forest on a cliff ledge east of the Cove, and west the crumpled strata of Stair Hole, the hollowed Purbeck mass of Durdle Door; and the chalk cliffs of Mupe Bay to the east and from St Oswald's Bay to White Nothe (including Bats Head) westward. Take the path over green sea turf between the cliff edges and the higher downland.

Lulworth Castle was built in the 16th century by Lord Bindon, and became the home of the Roman Catholic family of Weld. St Mary's Church, East Lulworth, is in the castle grounds. Said to be the first Roman Catholic church built in England since the Reformation. Home, until 1926, of the famous illuminated Luttrell Psalter, now in British Museum.
10 m. S. of Bere Regis.

LYME REGIS, *Dorset.* **15**, 58.
The last Dorset coast town before Devonshire, an uncontaminated little resort and harbour combined. Charming houses along the miniature sea front from which you walk to the Cobb, the curving stone pier protecting the harbour. See the fossils in the little museum, and the Geological Society's window in the church to Mary Anning, the 'eminent female fossilist' who found the first ichthyosaurus and plesiosaurus in the coastal Lias towards Charmouth. Recall Jane Austen and Louisa Musgrove's fall on the Cobb; and visit the landslips further west in Devon between Pinhay and Dowlands. Perhaps only Tenby in Pembrokeshire has more to offer the discerning as a coastal resort.
24 m. W. of Dorchester.

LYNDHURST, *Hampshire*
The New Forest can be explored from this peaceful but not remarkable town, where the Forest cattle wander about the main road to Southampton. Note the King's House, where the verderers of the Forest hold their courts; and the

Gothic Revival church by William White (1860), with a wall painting by Leighton, glass by Burne-Jones and Rossetti, and the marble effigy to the wife of S. P. Cockerell with *art nouveau* railings (*c.* 1880). Mrs. Hargreaves, the Alice of *Alice in Wonderland*, is buried in a family vault in the graveyard.
9 m. S.W. of Southampton.

MAIDEN CASTLE, *Dorset*. **9**, 16.
Vast prehistoric fortified site outside Dorchester. 2½ m. S.W. of Dorchester.

MARLBOROUGH, *Wiltshire*
A warm and dignified little downland market town, consisting in the main of one long street of good buildings, tea shops (where the visitor may study English schoolboys from Marlborough College out with their parents), book shops, antique shops, etc. The Mop Fair is still held in the High Street. A good centre for the Downs, Avebury, Wansdyke, etc. Savernake Forest, just outside the town on the London road, has sylvan glades and ancient timber.
27 m. N. of Salisbury.

MATTINGLEY, *Hampshire*
The odd little 15th-century church is made of wood and brick, with timber arcading inside.
5 m. N. of Odiham.

MERE, *Wiltshire*
One of the forgotten little towns of Wessex. Its grey isolation has never been invaded by the railway and the town has an undamaged unity, even if its buildings, one by one, are not remarkable. The mainly 15th-century church is spaciously divided by oak screens of great delicacy. Note the brasses and the early 19th-century wall tablet in the chancel depicting a coffin. The poet William Barnes kept his first school in the Chantry House near the church. Elaborate iron work outside the Ship Inn. There is a fine descent into Mere from Salisbury Plain. 8 m. N.W. of Shaftesbury.

MILTON ABBAS and MILTON ABBEY, *Dorset*. 54.
The Earl of Dorchester made this model village in the 18th century. The old village was around the Abbey out of which Chambers contrived him a grey mansion (now a hospital). The Abbey church (14th- and 15th-centuries) has a splendid interior of gleaming white and yellow. Note in it the ivory triptych, Carlini's memorial to Lord and Lady Milton, the tomb of the Danish international banker Baron Hambro who had a financial share in establishing Italian independence and the curious shell and angel font in white marble by the Danish sculptor A. Jerichau. 8½ m. S.W. of Blandford.

NETLEY ABBEY, *Hampshire*
Well situated ruins of a Cistercian house above Southampton Water. Much (mainly 13th-century) remains of the abbey church, the visiting abbot's lodging, the chapter house, the parlour and the vestry, etc. 3½ m. S.E. of Southampton.

NEW FOREST, *Hampshire*. **31**.
The Forest needs exploring on foot, at length. The motorist, save for a gladed road here and there, will find it disappointing and will wonder why so much fuss is made about its beauties of heath and woodland. Lyndhurst (q.v.) is a good centre; and for forest primaevalism, explore Whitley Wood (oak) on the right of A 337 south of Lyndhurst, the yews of Sloden Enclosure reached by a walk across open land from Fritham, or the woods N.W. of Burley Lodge. The Rufus Stone, marking the supposed spot where William Rufus, King of England, was killed by an arrow in 1100, lies west of Cadnam, in the angle of B 3079 and A 31, in a good forest area. The Forest trees include oak, beech, yew, holly and in certain areas conifer crops.

OLD SARUM, *Wiltshire*. **5**, 26.
See under Salisbury.

OSMINGTON, *Dorset*
Pretty village with a stone church and parsonage alongside where Constable stayed with his parson friend Fisher and painted. His *Weymouth Bay* (National Gallery) probably painted from sketches at Osmington Mills.
4½ m. N. E. of Weymouth.

PEWSEY, *Wiltshire*
The small town of Pewsey is rather less interesting than the Vale of Pewsey, a fertile greensand interlude between the chalk of the Marlborough Downs and the chalk of Salisbury Plain. There are moving views as one descends into the Vale over either slope, especially from above Alton Barnes. Note Knap Hill, with its causewayed camp, as on Windmill Hill at Avebury (q.v.).
7 m. S.W. of Marlborough.

PILSDON PEN, *Dorset*
909 feet, this great flat-topped hill is the highest point of Dorset, dominant in an area of long views over the clay vale of Marshwood and fine scenery. An Iron Age camp on the summit. Lewesdon Hill, thickly wooded (National Trust) is its neighbour. Under the western slopes of Pilsdon Pen, the plain mansion of Racedown, once occupied by William and Dorothy Wordsworth. 9. m. N.E. of Lyme Regis.

POOLE, *Dorset*
The town breezily faces Poole Harbour and is worth visiting despite Bournemouth suburbanism for the harbour views, the 18th-century Town Hall and Customs House, the 1820 church, the fossils in the museum and the curious dark and hollow medieval house of Scaplen's Court. Pottery is still made from the clay of the heaths between Corfe and Wareham.
5¼ m. W. of Bournemouth.

PORTCHESTER CASTLE, *Hampshire*. 21, **36**.
The Roman *Portus Adurni*. Roman fort, of which

Wardour Old Castle.

some of the walls and bastions are unusually well-preserved, also medieval castle and church. One of the historic places of Wessex which should on no account be missed. Now in charge of the Ministry of Works, which publishes a brief pamphlet of its history. 6 m. N.W. of Portsmouth.

PORTESHAM, *Dorset*
Village near Abbotsbury (q.v.) under the hills. Long barrows and stone circles within easy reach on foot. Two miles east a little medieval chapel at Corton Farm.
7 m. N.W. of Weymouth.

ISLE OF PORTLAND, *Dorset*. **16**, 59.
This is the crude rockery from which St Paul's Cathedral in London was contrived – quarries and quarrymen, wind, fog, fossils, wild flowers, sharp cliffs, a small museum, and the mansion of Pennsylvania Castle (1800) designed by Wyatt for the grandson of William Penn. Relics of the Penn family here include a portrait of William Penn. Portland is reached by a road from Weymouth along the Chesil Bank (q.v.), crossing the one narrow link between the Fleet and the sea.

PORTSMOUTH, *Hampshire*. **40**, **43**.
This naval town, the companion of the civil Southampton, does in our day what Portchester did for the Romans. There is much to see beyond the obvious attraction of Nelson's *Victory* in the Dockyard; and in spite of severe bombing in the war, which played havoc with the Old Town. In the High Street note the house in which Felton murdered the Duke of Buckingham in 1628, the Landport Gate, and the Square Tower on which there is a gilt bust of Charles I. There is much of interest in the parish church, which for some years now has been raised to cathedral standing, including a monument to the Duke of Buckingham. The museum house in which Dickens was born (1812) is in Commercial Road. 70 m. S.W. of London.

PUDDLETOWN, *Dorset*
Here is an impressive though small church with good fittings and a side chapel of alabaster effigies affectingly redolent of medievalism. Note old canvas fire buckets. 5½ m. N.E. of Dorchester.

ISLE OF PURBECK, *Dorset*. **45**, 50, 58.
See also under Swanage and Kimmeridge Bay.

RAMSBURY, *Wiltshire*
A good village with a history of ancient importance as an Anglo-Saxon see. Interesting monuments in the church including a wigged, recumbent figure of Sir William Jones (1631-1682), the Attorney-General who prosecuted in the Popish Plot, called by Dryden in *Absalom and Achitophel* the

'Bull-fac'd Jonas, who could statutes draw
To mean rebellion and make treason law.'

6 m. N.E. of Marlborough.

ROMSEY, *Hampshire*. 30.
The squat, strong abbey church dominates the town in point of interest. Romsey Abbey was founded in the 10th century. The church is mainly Norman of the 12th century. Note the post-Saxon rood outside, the reredos in the north transept, the battle carved on one of the Norman capitals, the Saxon rood *inside* the church, and the 15th-century cope.
10 m. S.W. of Winchester.

SALISBURY, *Wiltshire*. **5**, **29**, 45.
After Winchester, the second city of Wessex. The cathedral, set in its wide green close, is all of a piece, built between 1220 and 1260. From a distance the first sign of Salisbury is the spire of the cathedral rising over dark hills. Note the rich effect of the combination of grey stone and polished black or dark brown marble from the Wessex Isle of Purbeck (q.v.) – peculiarly striking in the nave and the choir. Do not miss the Lady Chapel, the chapter house, or the cloisters, the remaining chantries, the effigies, and 18th- and 19th-century monuments (including Rysbrack's monument to Lord Wyndham). There is much else of interest in Salisbury of various periods from the middle ages, around the close and in the city (the medieval George Inn, for example), though Salisbury is less architecturally rich than Winchester. There is a notable secondhand bookshop by one of the gates into the close and the museum in St Anne's Street has fine archaeological collections which help one to an understanding of prehistoric Wiltshire and Wessex in general. The 15th-century Hall of John Halle, a wealthy wool merchant, is a reminder of how Salisbury gained its wealth from the vast sheep walks of Salisbury Plain.

Old Sarum, on a chalk hill at the outskirts of the city, was abandoned bit by bit in the Middle Ages. The great earthworks, the remains of the Norman castle, the outline in the turf of the Norman cathedral make Old Sarum one of the most fascinating antiquities of Wessex.
82½ m. S.W. of London.

SAVERNAKE FOREST, *Wiltshire*
See Marlborough.

SELBORNE, *Hampshire*
The village in the 'hanger' country – hangers are sharp, tree-covered descents – where the 18th-century naturalist Gilbert White was born, lived, observed and died. Selborne Hill, behind The Wakes, Gilbert White's home, now belongs to the National Trust. In Selborne church, a stone with 'G. W. 1793' lies over his grave. There is a memorial window to him of St Francis and the birds. Gilbert White's brother gave the altar painting, ascribed to the 16th-century painter, Jan Mostaert, of the Adoration of the Three Kings. 8¼ m. N. of Petersfield.

SHAFTESBURY, *Dorset*. **22**.
The lofty site of this small town on a ridge suggests a prehistoric antiquity. Nothing but the foundations are left of the great abbey. The town is isolated and quiet and has good buildings, especially the Grosvenor Hotel. The vast and odd Chevy Chase sideboard in the hotel dining room was exhibited at the Great Exhibition of 1851. Look at steep, cobbled Gold Hill, stroll along Park Walk, and gaze out from Bimport over the Vale of Blackmore, of which William Barnes was a native and which he describes so often in his poems. 13 m. N. of Blandford.

SHERBORNE, *Dorset*
An abbey town of mellow stone. The Abbey Church is partly Norman, mainly 15th-century. Note the luxurious architecture of the choir, the fan-vaulting, Pope's epitaph to two children of Lord Digby. Those who have tender memories of Sir Thomas Wyatt's poem 'They flee from me who sometime did me seek' may like to know that Wyatt is supposed to lie somewhere in the church. He certainly died at Sherborne in 1541. The ancient school associated with the abbey has good buildings. Also girls' public school. 5½ m. E. of Yeovil.

SHERBORNE ST JOHN, *Hampshire*
The Vyne, in this parish, is one of the best mansions in the county, Tudor with 17th-century additions. In the Tombhouse (1765) attached to the old chapel of the Vyne there is a splendid marble monument by Banks to Chaloner Chute, Speaker of the House of Commons. There are excellent monuments and brasses in the parish church.
2 m. N. of Basingstoke.

SILCHESTER, *Hampshire*. 20.
Founded by Atrebates, the Roman walls still stand. The little church in the corner of the walled enclosure has a Tudor pulpit and a dark air of unspoiled antiquity. 10 m. N. of Basingstoke.

SILTON, *Dorset*
Little visited, this lonely church has a magnificently involved monument to Sir Hugh Wyndham (1603–1684).
3¼ m. N.W. of Gillingham.

SOUTHAMPTON, *Hampshire*. **37**, 55, 60.
Like its neighbour Portsmouth, Southampton was badly damaged in air-raids, which have given archaeologists a rare chance to discover more of the Saxon town which succeeded the Roman *Clausentum*, at Bitterne across the Itchen. The medieval walls and towers (especially the Arcades) should be seen, the Norman House, the Hospital of St Julian, the 14th-century Wool House, the carved marble font (Norman) in St Michael's Church, and the Tudor House, which is now a museum. In the modern Civic Centre there is a municipal art gallery with an

The *Vecta*, an Isle of Wight steamer.

unusually good collection of paintings, recently assembled.

75½ m. S.W. of London.

STEEPLE, *Dorset*
For the 18th-century folly of Grange Arch see p. 50. 5 m. S. of Wareham.

STEVENTON, *Hampshire*
Piety may demand a visit to this village, where Jane Austen was born to the rector's wife in 1775, in a rectory which no longer exists. Here as a young girl she wrote *Pride and Prejudice* and *Northanger Abbey*, before the family moved to Bath in 1801. See also Chawton.

7 m. S.W. of Basingstoke.

STINSFORD, *Dorset*. 51.
Thomas Hardy's heart and his wives' remains in the churchyard. Hardy's birthplace at Higher Bockhampton, no great way off, is worth a visit even apart from its associations.

2 m. N.E. of Dorchester.

STONEHENGE, *Wiltshire*. 14–16.
Premier prehistoric monument of Wessex and Europe. See also Woodhenge nearby.

10 m. N. of Salisbury.

STOURHEAD, *Wiltshire*. 48, **65**.
A National Trust property: Palladian mansion, with a fine view to Salisbury Plain and a collection of pictures and furniture, and above all the 18th-century landscape garden, with grotto, temples, lakes, etc. 3 m. N.W. of Mere.

STRATFIELD SAYE, *Hampshire*
The mansion, park and estate of Stratfield Saye were given by the nation to the Duke of Wellington in gratitude for Waterloo. The Wellington Column is appropriately reached by an avenue of the Californian *Sequoia gigantea*, the world's largest tree, first called Wellingtonia in honour of the Duke (though Americans called the tree Washingtonia). The classical church (1784) contains Wellington and other family monuments. 7 m. N.E. of Basingstoke.

STUDLAND, DORSET.
Resort village with good sands and dark heaths and notable Norman Church.

8½ m. S.W. of Bournemouth.

SWANAGE, *Dorset*. **22**.
The grey capital of the Isle of Purbeck from which the quarries, surface and underground, the bleak Purbeck uplands, the Tilly Whim Caves, the savage cliffs towards St Aldhem's Head may be explored. On no account miss Winspit and Chapman's Pool and Hounstout Cliff. For Purbeck Stone and Marble see p. 58. Steamers to Bournemouth make a lovely cut across blue Swanage Bay backed by gleaming white cliffs. 11¾ m. S.W. of Bournemouth.

TISBURY, *Wiltshire*
The remarkable thing at Tisbury (where Sir John Davies, the Elizabethan author of *Nosce Teipsum* was born) is Place Farm, a grange of the abbesses of Shaftesbury, where the outer and inner gatehouses, the great thatched tithe barn and the farmhouse remain from the 15th century. 8 m. N.E. of Shaftesbury.

TITCHFIELD, *Hampshire*
A rewarding little town for its houses, its church and the remains of Titchfield Abbey (cared for by the Ministry of Works). The remains are overpowered by the Tudor mansion which Lord Chancellor Wriothesley built from the stones of the abbey church. His splendidly

Lulworth Castle, Dorset.

pompous memorial (1582) is in the parish church. 9¾ m. S.E. of Southampton.

TOLLARD ROYAL, *Wiltshire*
Here, in Cranborne Chase, on the edge of Dorset, lived the eccentric General Pitt-Rivers (memorial in the church). Hereabouts Pitt-Rivers, one of the founders of modern archaeological excavation, explored Belgic and Romano-British village sites and the great rampart and ditch of Bokerley Dyke, probably a defence against stock-raiders of the 4th century A.D. About a mile away is the Pitt-Rivers Museum among the fields at Farnham, over the Dorset border, containing the results of his excavations, excellent collections of primitive sculpture, Benin bronzes, china, bygones, etc. Something can be seen through the fence of the Larmer Grounds, no longer open, somewhat eccentrically laid out by the General as a civilizing influence for the masses. 6½ m. S.E. of Shaftesbury.

TOLPUDDLE, *Dorset*. 52.
The home of the Tolpuddle Martyrs.
7 m. E. of Dorchester.

WANSDYKE, *Wiltshire*. 23, 25.

WARDOUR CASTLE, *Wiltshire*. **87**.
The New Castle at Wardour is a classical mansion of 1768, now belonging to the Society of Jesus. The Old Castle nearly a mile S.E. (now cared for by the Ministry of Works) was built in 1393, besieged in the Civil War and partly destroyed. The fascination of these ruins is increased by the romantic garden laid out (early 19th-century) by Lord Arundell, complete with cedars, a Gothic garden house and grottoes by the Wiltshire grotto builder Josiah Lane who made the grottoes for Beckford at Fonthill (q.v.) and in other English gardens.
12½ m. W. of Salisbury.

WAREHAM, *Dorset*. 30.
Well-built, sleepy little town of great antiquity. A small Saxon church with reclining figure of T. E. Lawrence. Also the large Lady St Mary's Church is worth a visit on its own account and for details including the figured font (12th-century) in lead. The black heights of Purbeck loom to the S.W.
9¾ m. N.W. of Swanage.

WEYMOUTH, *Dorset*
Beaches and sea front are crowded in summer, but there is more to Weymouth than the obvious attractions of a summer resort. Above all there is the harbour, with its medley of boats and yachts, the quays where the boats leave for the Channel Islands; and on the fringe the naval Portland Harbour within its huge breakwaters. The neighbouring Isle of Portland (q.v.), Chesil Bank and the Fleet sternly contrast with the coloured, crowded beaches. Note the statue of George III (1809) on the esplanade. His holiday at Weymouth in 1789 greatly helped it as a resort. Portraits in the Town Hall and the *Last Supper* by the unjustly neglected artist Sir James Thornhill in St Mary's church.
8 m. S. of Dorchester.

WHITCHURCH CANONICORUM, *Dorset*.
A fine upstanding church in the Marshwood Vale with a 15th-century tower. The fragmentary stone shrine contains relics of St Wite or Candida. 5½ m. W. of Bridport.

ISLE OF WIGHT. **27**.
The Isle of Wight, reached from Lymington, Southampton and Portsmouth, is a world on its own admirably varied in scenery, with low green shores towards Hampshire, shores broken with landslips to the S. and S.E. and vertical chalk cliffs of much grandeur stretching westward to the Needles. There are chalk downs and valleys, low, rich farmland, narrow 'chines', or wooded clefts, running down to the English Channel. The Island has long been a holiday resort, made popular in the last century by Queen Victoria and Prince Albert – a popularity reflected in villas and mansions, hotels, the holiday towns of Ventnor, Shanklin, Sandown and Ryde, and latterly in holiday camps and tea gardens. For some tastes it is likely to be too crowded in the summer months. Perhaps it is at its best in spring, early summer and autumn.

The most notable building in the Island is Carisbrooke Castle, partly Norman on a Roman site. It is dramatic and well repays a visit. Churches worth visiting include Shorwell (wall painting, pulpit, and a reredos taken from the Icelandic church at Thingvellir), Brading (note especially the wooden effigies of the Oglanders), Godshill for the Worsley monuments and the wall painting of the Crucifixion, and Shalfleet.

Swinburne is buried outside the mid-19th-century church at Bonchurch by Ventnor. For the curious church at Whippingham, designed by Prince Albert, Queen Victoria's Osborne

House and the Swiss Cottage, see pp. 47–48.

The celebrated Blackgang Chine has been ruined by landslips, though the Bazaar is worth visiting for its mixed flavour of Early Victorianism and the motor-coach age. The National Trust owns the fine downs between Tennyson's Farringford House and the sea. A curious Trust property is the minute 18th-century town hall of Newtown, isolated among trees and fields.

The best of the towns are Ryde, Ventnor (for its Victorian and Edwardian flavour), the older cottage portion of Shanklin, and Yarmouth, unspoilt and breezily open to the Solent. Note the Tudor castle at Yarmouth, which defended the entrance to the Solent, and in the church the monument to Admiral Sir Robert Holmes, commander of the fleet which took New York from the Dutch in August 1664.

WILTON, *Wiltshire*. 48.
Small town appended to Wilton House (the Earl of Pembroke), on the site of the ancient abbey. The House is partly Tudor, partly Palladian by Inigo Jones and John Webb, partly neo-Gothic by Wyatt. Superb rooms, notable pictures by Lucas van Leyden, Van der Goes, Van Dyck, etc., and famous landscape garden. Wilton itself is a carpet-making town with a long history. The fascinatingly ostentatious church (1844) in the Italian Lombard style contains old glass, part of a 13th-century altar from St Maria Maggiore in Rome, and among the memorials a powerfully intimidating bust of one of the 18th-century Earls of Pembroke.

3½ m. W. of Salisbury.

WIMBORNE, *Dorset*
Thread the town to the Minster and wait for the coloured hammer-boy on the tower to strike one of the quarter hours. The clock and orrery inside are medieval. There is much of interest in this huge murky church including the Library and the effigy tomb of John Beaufort, Duke of Somerset (1403–1444).

10 m. S.E. of Blandford.

WIMBORNE ST. GILES, *Dorset*
A notable classical church (1732) with monuments of historic interest to the Earls of Shaftesbury – including Rysbrack's bust of the great Sir Anthony Ashley Cooper, the 1st Earl (1621–1683), statesman and as 'the curst Achitophel' one of Dryden's victims in *Absalom and Achitophel:*

'In friendship false, implacable in hate
Resolved to ruin or to rule the state,'

and an Italian memorial to the third earl (1671–1713), philosopher and author of *The Characteristicks*. He died in Naples. The monument made for him there shows 'Polite literature mourning the death of her most distinguished votary.' In the grounds of the family seat, St Giles's House, there is a shell grotto of 1751.

2 m. S.W. of Cranborne.

WINCHESTER, *Hampshire*. 28, 45, **57**.
A city with a medieval, Saxon, Roman and pre-Roman past; and glamorous to match. It was capital of the Saxon kingdom of Wessex and in Norman days, with London, twin capital of England. The long cathedral has Norman transepts and a Gothic nave, and a mainly Norman crypt. There are many objects to examine in this immense ecclesiastical cavern – the various chantries of the 14th and 15th centuries, the Lady Chapel, the reredos and the choir stalls, the 12th-century font, the royal relic chests, the wall paintings in the chapel of the Holy Sepulchre, statues of James I and Charles I, the tomb of William Rufus, memorials of all periods (including work by Flaxman and Chantrey) and the grave of Jane Austen, who died in a house in College Street (tablet).

The other buildings of special note are those of Winchester College, the celebrated Great Hall (13th-century) part of the castle of the kings of England, the Guildhall (1713), the Westgate and the Kingsgate, and many houses from the Middle Ages to the 18th century. But second in attraction to the cathedral is St Cross Hospital, with its church, dating from the 12th century, its quadrangles, hall, and the houses of the poor brethren maintained by ancient medieval charity. On St Catherine's Hill, the pre-Roman camp may have been the Belgic town preceding Roman Winchester. There is a more or less square mizmaze on the hill, one of those labyrinths descending, so it seems, from an ancient ritual game (see also Breamore).

63 m. S.W. of London.

WOLVERTON, *Hampshire*
Wolverton should be visited for its classical brick church (1717) in which much of the original church furniture survives.

7 m. N.W. of Basingstoke.

WORBARROW BAY, *Dorset*
Geologically a repetition of Lulworth Cove on a bigger scale. The Portland wall is cut between Worbarrow Tout and Mupe Rocks; and the sea is eating into the chalk at Arish Mell. The cliffs of the bay are capped at 567 feet by the Iron Age camp of Flowers Barrow.

2½ m. E. (by footpath) from Lulworth.

SOME RECENT BOOKS ON WESSEX

Arkell, W. J. *Geology of the Country round Weymouth, Swanage, Corfe and Lulworth.* H.M.S.O. 1947. 17s. 6d.

Benfield, Eric. *Purbeck Shop.* (The author began as a Purbeck quarryman.) Cambridge University Press. 1940. 15s.

Brentnall, H. C., and Carter, C. C. *The Marlborough Country.* Oxford University Press. 1932. 3s. 6d.

Chatwin, C. P. *British Regional Geology: The Hampshire Basin and adjoining areas.* H.M.S.O. 1948. 2s. 6d.

Cook, G. H. *Portrait of Salisbury Cathedral.* Phoenix House. 1950. 12s. 6d.

Cunnington, M. E. *Introduction to the Archaeology of Wiltshire.* (Excellent for Stonehenge, Avebury, etc.) G. Simpson (Devizes). 1933.

Darrell Reed, Trelawney. *The Rise of Wessex.* Methuen. 1947. 18s.

Davies, G. M. *The Dorset Coast: A Geological Guide.* T. Murby. 1935. 6s.

De Sélincourt, A. *Isle of Wight.* Paul Elek. 1948. 9s. 6d.

Good, Ronald. *The Old Roads of Dorset.* Longmans (Dorchester). 1940.

Grinsell, L. V. *White Horse Hill and the Surrounding Country.* St Catherine Press. 1939. 4s. 6d.

Lonsley, J. E. *Wild Flowers of Chalk and Limestone.* Collins' New Naturalist Series. 1950. 21s.

Marples, M. *White Horses and Other Hill Figures.* Country Life, 1949. 21s.

Massingham, H. J. *The English Downland.* Batsford. 1949. 12s. 6d.

Meade Falkner, J. *Moonfleet.* Edward Arnold. Reprinted 1949. 3s. 9d. (A brilliant and too little known adventure story of the Dorset coast in which the bizarre scenery, cliff quarries, etc. are prominent.)

Rannie, A. *The Winchester Countryside.* Allen & Unwin. 1948. 8s. 6d.

Vesey-Fitzgerald, Brian. *Hampshire and the Isle of Wight.* Robert Hale. 1949. 15s.

White, Gilbert. *The Natural History of Selborne.* (First published in 1789.) Cresset. 1947. 8s. 6d.

Detailed guides to Hampshire, Dorset and Wiltshire are available in the *Little Guide* series (the Hampshire volume is excellent), and to Hampshire and the Isle of Wight together and Wiltshire and Dorset together in the sketchier *Penguin Guides;* but it is well to supplement these with *Murray's Handbooks* of the nineteenth century, the best and fullest guides to the individual counties ever published. Though long out of print, it is not difficult to find secondhand copies. Details of everything which belongs to the National Trust will be found in the inexpensive *National Trust: List of Properties*, 1950. See also *National Trust Guide: Buildings*, by J. Lees-Milne, 1931, and the *National Trust Guide: Places of Natural Beauty*, by D. M. Matheson, 1950. Those who are interested in the rich archaeological remains of Wessex will find an excellent gazetteer of the things most worth visiting in *Prehistoric Britain*, by J. and C. Hawkes. Chatto & Windus. 1948.

MAPS

Excellent maps for the whole of Britain are published by the Ordnance Survey and by Bartholomew. The most useful for travellers are the one-inch and the quarter-inch series. In addition, a series of special maps is published by the Ordnance Survey, each covering Britain in two sheets on the scale of 1/625,000 (about ten miles to one inch). This series includes: 'Coal and Iron', 'Land Classification', 'Land Utilization', 'Railways', 'Types of Farming', 5s. per sheet; and 'Solid Geology', 12s. 6d. per sheet.